ESSAYS IN RELIGION

By EMMA FRIEDER

Altar Fires

Essays in Religion

ESSAYS
IN RELIGION

by Emma Frieder

An Exposition-Testament Book

EXPOSITION PRESS   NEW YORK

291
F913

EXPOSITION PRESS INC.

50 Jericho Turnpike   Jericho, New York 11753

FIRST EDITION

Library of Congress Catalog Card Number: 68-24888

EP 46850

INSCRIPTION

THE Bible has been for so many centuries the Word of God that its significance as the full expression of a nation's life has been obscured. We have a book of literary value whose oral traditions go back to Babylon's youth and Egypt's maturity; a book whose records often parallel the monuments of the old empires; a report of an early political experiment carried on for a thousand years to prove the theory that "right makes might"; and an illustration of evolution in history from the crudest to the finest spiritual and moral life. We may follow a path of thought as broad and clear as the moon on the waters; or, to use the familiar biblical metaphor, the light, faint at first, grows and grows into the perfection of day.

CONTENTS

ESSAYS IN RELIGION

AN ESSAY IN RELIGION

A Symposium

THE COMMON BELIEFS

THE earliest literature of a people is always sacred. It preserves whatever is known of national origins and is the mainspring of pride of race.

In the Introduction to the *Sacred Books of the East,* F. Max Müller lists, in addition to the Bible, six considerable and original bodies of sacred literature, all from the East—the books of the Brahmans, the Buddhists, the Zoroastrians, of the Confucianists, the Taoists, the Moslems—and the fragmentary remains of Babylonian, Assyrian, and Egyptian religion, especially the multifarious Egyptian *Book of the Dead.* Like the Egyptian Memnon, the voice of God was heard at the dawn, and without hint or suspicion of priestly fraud.

In these religious writings are preserved, almost without a word in exception, the earliest literary monuments of antiquity. The religions founded on them are still the religions of the world. The religions of the Egyptians and the Babylonians persist in a debased mysticism—magic—and in the occult sciences. All the roots run deep. Men's beliefs are not drawn out of air.

The sacred texts unfold the love of God as an indigenous growth of the human heart, although often a more than human wit would need to untangle the tares from the golden grain of reason: still the love of God—not the mere coordinate love of Truth and Right, but the love of God—inextricably rooted in the instinctive passions of men. God under many forms: God without form or attribute—the Indian Brahman or the Greek Absolute: God with a plenitude of attributes human and divine —the God of Israel: God with the highest degree of all attributes —the God of Islam. The Moslem counts off on a rosary the ninety-nine attributes of God, and first or last, he names the Name that, like God himself, never changes.

The ideal belief subsists by the side of a popular nature religion and magic, as the pre-Exilic prophets had always to meet a stubborn idolatry. Perhaps the esoteric doctrine revealed by Osiris, "the sovereign Intelligence," to Hermes, the Egyptian Thoth, scribe of the gods in his desire "to behold the source of beings . . . and to know God," was the secret revealed to the initiated the world over: "There is only one law and He who works is One." ("And this is God, the All.")[1] The greatest thought that ever came into the mind of man was not the exclusive possession of one race, or of advanced races alone. Some of the most primitive tribes know the All-Father, self-existing, all-creating.

The Babylonian Code of Hammurabi, the oldest extant, is not a religious law, like the Jewish Book of the Covenant: still, the oath is taken before the gods, and the exact provisions, covering a great diversity of practical social matters, are made in reverence to God, and with the intention of establishing peace and justice throughout the empire:

[1] "The Vision of Hermes," quoted from Brian Brown, *Wisdom of the Egyptians*, p. 272. Version in parentheses quoted from *Hastings' Encyclopedia of Religion and Ethics*, VI, 629.

Anu and Bel called by name me, Hammurapi, the exalted prince, who feared God, to bring about the rule of righteousness in the land, to destroy the wicked and the evil doers; so that the strong should not harm the weak; so that I should rule over the black-headed people like Shamash (the Sun god) and enlighten the land, to further the well-being of mankind.[2]

In the Chinese rationalistic religion of conduct (propriety) and character, the learning of the sage is the endowment of Heaven, "the lofty One who is on high." In the Books of History (*Shu Ching*) and of Poetry (*Shih Ching* [or *King*]) of the older scriptures Heaven is a personal God (Ti, or Shang-Ti).

Sincerity, as expounded by the disciple of Confucius, in *The Doctrine of the Mean,* is the immanent Deity. "Sincerity is the way of Heaven."

"There is no image of Him whose name is Great Glory," exclaims the enraptured Brahman.

The Zoroastrian invokes the Almighty: "O Ahura Mazda, most beneficent Spirit, Maker of the material world, thou Holy One"; or more briefly: "O Maker of the material world, thou Holy One."

Xenophanes in Elea, Sicily (Magna Graecia), an exile from Colophon, is called by Aristotle the first "of these partisans of the One" (*Metaphysics* I.5). The Eleatic in Plato's dialogue *The Sophist* refers to Xenophanes' successor as "my father Parmenides."

When Parmenides and Zeno, in Athens for the religious festival, the Great Panathenaea, discuss with Socrates how the individuals participate in the Ideas (how things of sense and perception partake of the ideal, eternal forms), Socrates, then very young, greets them with banter. They have said the same thing two ways: Parmenides, "The all is one"; Zeno, "There is no many."

To Plato "God is the measure of all things" (*Laws* IV.2)— of the Beautiful, the Good, the True, the Just—always and alto-

---

[2] *Sacred Books and Early Literature of the East,* I (Part IV), 114 ("Letters and Inscriptions of Hammurapi," trans. L. W. King).

gether lovely, from whom the soul comes and to whom it returns. The Eternal Ideas vaguely harmonize the discrepancy between the ethical unity of God and the dualism that runs through the whole spiritual as well as the phenomenal world.

Plato's piety increased with the years. At the end of his days he wrote:

> God is the natural and worthy object of our most serious and blessed endeavors, for man, as I said before, is made to be the plaything of God, and this, truly considered, is the best of him; wherefore also every man and woman should walk seriously, and pass life in the noblest of pastimes, and be of another mind from what they are at present. (*Laws* VII)

Aristotle quotes Xenophanes: "The One is God" (*Metaphysics*). The "Master of those who know" chants the praises of the Everlasting, the Prime Mover, himself unmoved—the One "with whom is no variableness, neither shadow of turning," as James puts it.

> If, then, God is always in that good state in which we sometimes are, this compels our wonder; and if in a better this compels it yet more. And God *is* in a better state. And life also belongs to God; for the actuality of thought is life, and God is that actuality; and God's self-dependent[3] actuality is life most good and eternal. We say therefore that God is a living being, eternal, most good, so that life and duration continuous and eternal belong to God, for this *is* God. . . . The unmovable first mover is one both in definition[4] and in number. (*Metaphysics* XII.7:8)

And the trumpet blast from Zion answers the thunderclap from Sinai: "Hear, O Israel: the Lord our God, the Lord is One."

Mohammed only recalled the Arabians to the One God in back of the 360 gods in the Caaba. The chapter entitled "The Declaration of God's Unity" is said to be worth a third of the whole Koran. In the notes to chapter 112 or 113 George Sale gives an alternate translation in the rhythm of the original:

---

[3] According to another translation (Smith and Ross): "essential."
[4] *Ibid.*: "formula."

> Say, God is one God.
> He is the eternal.
> He hath naught begotten.
> He is not begotten.
> Like him there is none.

Hughes' *Dictionary of Islam* gives chapter 113:

> Say, He is God, One [God].
> God the Eternal.
> He begetteth not nor is begotten.
> And there is none equal unto Him.

* * *

In the Vedic hymns appears the idea of a supreme God among gods, under many names. ("For the Lord your God is a God of Gods, and Lord of Lords, a great God, a mighty and a terrible.")

We meet the hymn in the collection of the *Rig-Veda* to the Unknown God Ka—"Who." European scholars suspect it of being late—late in the Vedas—and date it 1000 B.C. Nor are the Vedic hymns primitive folk poetry, but the work of a settled priesthood.

In Ka ("Who") being and non-being meet. The concept of "the One who is" may be conversely stated as "the One who is not." Since attributes are accidents of mortality, pure non-being is not non-existence but freedom from accidents.

("Whose shadow is immortality, whose shadow is death.")

TO THE UNKNOWN GOD (KA—"WHO")[5]

1. In the beginning there arose the Golden Child (Hiranyagarbha); as soon as born, he alone was the lord of all that is. He established the earth and this heaven:—Who is the God to whom we shall offer sacrifice?

2. He who gives breath, he who gives strength, whose command all the bright gods revere, whose shadow is immortality, whose shadow is death:—Who is the God to whom we shall offer sacrifice?

[5] F. Max Müller (trans.), *Vedic Hymns* (*Sacred Books of the East*, XXXII, part I), X, hymn 121.VIII.7.3–4.

Legge argues from the primitive Chinese custom of sacrificing to ancestors the ancient belief in the continued existence of the dead. The mystic faith of Laocius (Lao-tzu) as presented in the brief *Tao Te King* (The Way and Virtue Book) and in the work of the disciple Chuang-tzu offers a definite certainty for the vague Confucian belief in immortality.

Felix Adler measures the conviction of immortality in the Indian against even the orthodox Christian's of today "as a mighty oak to a sapling willow." Neither Indian nor Egyptian ever required any proof of immortality. Neither ever thought of life as terminating. The *Book of the Dead* is the Book of Life Eternal.

Funerary pyramid texts, in part older than the dynasties, express the belief that the mummified great dead will "put on immortality," that he will reign as Osiris, who, himself a mortal, rose from the dead, or will abide a god with Re for the millions of years.

In the realistic metaphor of Mazdeism, Best Mind is Heaven, Worst Mind is Hell. The soul alone sees the Kinvat bridge. There the wicked, convicted of sin by their own evil consciences, are unable to keep footing on the narrow path, but plunge into the abyss where is the mouth of Hell, to dwell forever in the abode of the Lie. But the soul justified by Good Thoughts, Good Words, Good Deeds, conducted by Sraosha, Spirit of Piety—"the holy, strong Sraosha"—sustained by Conscience, the most desirable of maidens ("I was lovely and thou madest me still lovelier"), treads in security a broad highway that leads to the regions of Light.

The Pharisaic author of II Maccabees comments on Judas Maccabeus' offering for the sins of the dead: "If he had not been mindful of the resurrection it would have been superfluous and vain to pray for them" (12:43–45).

The creation narrative in Genesis, from the common Semitic stock, testifies to a primordial belief.

And the Lord God said, "Behold, the man is become as one of us, to know good and evil" [one of us in the House of the Gods]:

and now, lest he put forth his hand, and take also of the tree of life, and eat, and live forever [the presumptuous fellow would eat the fruit of the tree that the Immortals eat, and live like them forever]: therefore the Lord God sent him forth from the garden of Eden, to till the ground from whence he was taken.

So He drove out the man; and He placed at the east of the garden of Eden the cherubim, and the flaming sword which turned every way, to keep the way to the tree of life. (Gen. 3:22–24)

("Strait is the gate, and narrow is the way which leadeth unto life [Immortal Life]; and few there be that find it.")

The Jews used the figure of the fruit of the tree; the Indians, Iranians, Greeks, of the fire which is life.

The Indian Agni, eldest of the gods and youngest, priest in Heaven as on earth—for the gods offer sacrifices—is "the kind friend to men" like Prometheus. "The lovely one in the house," the fire that cheers the hearth, glows in the sun and in the heart of man. "He who is in the fire, and he who is in the heart, and he who is in the sun, they are one and the same" (*Upanishads*).

In the Iranian religion, fire became the symbol of a passionate purity, lambent as the god. The Greek Prometheus filched the fire of the Immortals for men, bringing down all the evils in Pandora's urn, with mitigating hope.

It is encouraging to reflect that once man had nothing good behind and only good in prospect, and he went ahead.

Man that vaulted the battlement of Heaven to filch the fire of the Immortals while they caroused . . . man that sat with his back against the holy tree and swore that he wouldn't move till he had what he wanted—the supreme and absolute enlightenment . . . man that stole the fruit of the tree of knowledge though it lost him Eden: if the Kingdom of Heaven is taken by the violent, he's got what it takes; his own eyes must see his God.

Homer dominates Greek religion as Moses does the Hebraic. The "wisest" of men paid with his life for supplanting the old gods with new divinities of his own. But Socrates has the faith that Homer lacks. He anticipates the pleasure of meeting the great in the next world, and, awaiting death, consoles his friends with hopes of a blessed immortality.

To Homer, Hades is the dreary land of shades, like the Babylonian Aralu and the Hebrew Sheol. Odysseus flatters Achilles, whom he meets on the visit to the underworld: "He was like a god on earth and now he rules among the dead."

> Speak not thus of death
> As if thou couldst console me...

"Better be slave on earth than lord among the dead."

Life is sweet, the more joyless the shadowy existence in the grim halls of the dread Proserpina. But old Priam cannot close his eyes in sleep, nor partake of food or wine, until he has recovered the body of Hector from Achilles for proper burial, that the soul may enter the dark House of Death.

The lordly poet of imperial Rome sees no higher vision. He comforts Octavia, sister of Augustus, mother of the young Marcellus, untimely dead: "The gods were envious." Against the harsh fates Virgil can only oppose the solace of hopeless tears.

> ... In your hands bring lilies aplenty.
> I will scatter the deep-dyed flowers. ...
> [There is no hope for man.]

The mind calls up a group of humble mourners in the heart of the Judean hills: "Said I not unto thee, that if thou wouldest believe, thou shouldest see the glory of God?"

The most ancient written records testify to the belief in God, in continued existence, and in a definitely attainable and permanent good. This good the Jews loved to call salvation. God can confer an everlasting salvation, since His is an everlasting love.

"No evil can happen to a good man," Socrates in his closing address reassures the friendly jurors, his true judges, "either in life or after death. He and his are not neglected by the gods; nor has

my own approaching end happened by mere chance." (*Apology*.)
Paul gives like assurance to the Romans: "We know that all
things work together for good to them that love God, to them
who are the called according to his purpose."

The *Symposium* of Plato traces the ascent of the soul from
earthly love to the true Beauty, the soul grown dear to God
and immortal, if mortal may be. The Christian experience is in-
dicated as salvation through faith in Jesus Christ, sanctification
through the gift of the Holy Spirit, glorification "when this
mortal shall have put on immortality."

The young man in the Gospels asks, "What good thing shall
I do, that I may have eternal life?"

All religions prescribe a mode of life by which the desired
good is to be reached. The Chinese religion of mysticism is named
the Way—the Tao. The Buddhist must follow the Path. "I am
the Way . . ." declares Jesus: "no man cometh unto the Father
but by me."

Jeremiah invited his contemporaries to stand and look back
at the old paths and inquire of them "the good way," which seems
always to be the middle way, the mean. Isaiah foresaw a highway
called the Way of Holiness. The Psalmist sings:

> Happy is the man whose strength is in Thee;
> In whose heart are the highways.

The Japanese speaks of Kodo—the Kingly Way: the Christian
monk of "the Royal Way of the holy Cross."

Paul approves the religious character of the Athenians, but
he shows them "a more excellent way." The philosophers' schools
of Greece were religious communities as much bent on formulating a rule or way of life as on understanding the constitution of
things. When Plato joined the company of the barefoot philosopher,
it was as if a youth of our day, fortunately placed, rarely endowed, should throw in his lot with the Salvation Army or some
ascetic brotherhood.

"He who offends against Heaven has none to whom he can

pray," counsels the most revered of sages. Soothill renders this much quoted aphorism: "If a man sin against Heaven he has nowhere left for prayer." In his whole arid heart there is not room for one aspiration. (*Analects of Confucius* III.xiii.2.)

In the early religious records of ancient Egypt we miss the familiar "I have sinned." In the entire *Book of the Dead* "the soul admits no sin."

The mummy wrested by archaeologists from his tomb was prepared to meet the Lord of the Dead, Osiris, in the judgment hall of the Two Truths—Justice and Right—to make a general declaration of innocence, to deny specifically before each of the forty-two gods sitting with him in judgment one moral sin. There under the eyes of Horus, the falcon god, the old jackal-headed god of graves, Anubis, conductor of the dead, weighs the heart against the Truth, the goddess Maat or her symbol, an ostrich feather; and the ibis-headed Thoth records his decision, while the terror-stricken defendant, fortified with potent charms and amulets, calls to the heart that he had from his mother not to belie his protestations of purity.

In the Babylonian penitential psalms the penitent is aware of having incurred divine disfavor, but calls upon the resources of magic to discover his misdeed. The object of his prayer is to escape the effect of the evil spell. Unlike the sober realization of the Hebrew Psalmist, who knows his transgression and prays to be delivered from his sin.

The Pious Ruler, the "Babylonian Job," laments that he has faithfully and joyfully served his god and his goddess, and is only bewildered by all that has come upon him. He does not comfort himself with the wonders of God's creation, or with the greatness of God in which Job builds his lasting home. Redemption to him means that the demons of disease have been routed by Marduk or Enlil in a mighty storm.[6]

As deep as the Hebrew consciousness of sin was the Persian's. The unconfessed sin was a trouble to him. The performance of the *patet* remitted the eternal but not the temporal penalties of

---

[6] *Sacred Books and Early Literature of the East*, I (Part VIII), 251–52 (Psalm) and 253–59 (Lament).

sin. The "false cleanser" and the "carrier alone" of the dead paid with his life, but his soul was saved. The sentence was executed with the repetition of the formulary:

> The man here has repented of all his evil thoughts, words, and deeds. If he has committed any other evil deed, it is remitted by his repentance: if he has committed no other evil deed, he is absolved by his repentance forever and ever. (*Vendidad* IX.III.49–50)

In the invigorating metaphor of the *Avesta*: "The religion of Mazda cleanses the faithful from every evil thought, word, and deed as a swift-rushing mighty wind cleanses the plain." (*Vendidad* VIII.V.30.)

The Homeric Greeks were happily unburdened by a sense of sin. As Helen passes along the wall of Troy, the two noble sages remark—so ancient that their voices are like grasshoppers':

> Small blame is theirs if both the Trojan knights
> And brazen-mailed Achaians have endured
> So long so many evils for the sake
> Of that one woman. She is wholly like
> In features to the deathless goddesses.

Priam has no reproach for her:

> Come, dear daughter, sit by me.
> Thou canst behold thy former husband hence,
> Thy kindred and thy friends: I blame thee not;
> The blame is with the immortals.

Helen answers:

> Dear second father, whom at once
> I fear and honor, would that cruel death
> Had overtaken me before I left,
> To wander with thy son . . .
>   the company
> Of friends I loved. But that was not to be;
> And now I pine and weep.

Andrew Lang says of Helen: "Her repentance is without remorse." Rather is her remorse without repentance—attrition, not contrition.

Iris invites Helen to watch the combat between Paris and Menelaus that will decide which is to possess her.

> And in the heart of Helen woke
> Dear recollections of her former spouse
> And of her home and kindred.

She went "shedding tender tears"—but not for the wantonness that doomed the lofty towers of Ilium. ("I hold thee not to blame; nay, I hold the gods to blame.") Helen would have derived small comfort from the chapter in the Koran entitled "Women."

> Verily repentance will be accepted with God, from those who do evil ignorantly and then repent speedily; unto them will God be turned: for God is knowing and wise. But no repentance shall be accepted from those who do evil until the time when death presenteth itself unto one of them and he saith, Verily, I repent now; nor unto those who die unbelievers: for them have we prepared a grievous punishment.

Safest is it to "ask pardon early in the morning." (K.3:17; 4:16–17.)

The first missionary religion, Buddhism, invents the term for conversion in the first stage of saintship, "the entrance into the current"—to be *au courant* with eternity—in Sanskrit *srotaapatti;* in Pali *sota(a)patti.*

John the Baptist heralds the Messiah with one foreword from Heaven—"Repent." Jesus comes into Galilee proclaiming the Kingdom—"Repent!"

Esau, who sold his birthright, lost his place in the Kingdom because "he found no way to change his mind" (no means of return to God); "when he would have inherited the blessing he was rejected: for he found no place of repentance, though he sought it carefully with tears."

The godly Enoch became "an example of repentance to all generations."

Jesus convicts his own generation in the prophetic sentence used against idols. They have eyes and see not, ears and hear not.

The people stultify themselves. "Lest they should see with their eyes, and hear with their ears, and should understand with their heart, and should be converted, and I should heal them."

God calls all men to repentance as the way of Heaven. Even the righteous Job repented his presumption before God; for the stars are not pure in His sight, nor His angels innocent.

"I have sinned against the Lord," readily acknowledged King David before the denunciation of the prophet.

Happy the man and happy the nation that can still say: "I have sinned before God." Happy the man and happy the nation that can still hear the word of absolution from on high: "The Lord also hath put away thy sin."

RELIGIOUS SPECULATION

THE metaphysical inquiry into the nature of reality and being and the validity of perception (How do I know?) animates the Upanishads of Brahmanism and Greek philosophy. The Jewish writers barely touched on the metaphysical. Their overwhelming interest was in practical morality.

Moses addressed the children of Israel in the name of the God of their fathers—the "I Am That I Am." "I AM hath sent me unto you." Isaiah spoke of "the High and Lofty One inhabiting eternity, whose name is 'Holy.' "

> I dwell in the high and holy place,
> With him also that is of a contrite and humble spirit,
> To revive the spirit of the humble,
> And to revive the heart of the contrite ones. (Isa. 57:15)

Still it was a small world that the Jews inhabited, the spiritual landscape intimate and familiar. Indian philosophy comprehended worlds upon worlds, multiplied existences, innumerable vast cycles of time. The Jews expressed their simple ideas with unmistakable clarity and with unsurpassed variety and beauty of imagery. The ideas of Indian philosophy are, partly from their nature, vague; and their pessimism may spring, as Barth suggests, not from world-weariness but from daring speculation.

Since even in the dualist system of Indian philosophy the only existence or reality is Brahman, the Absolute, or *That,* it follows logically enough in the monist system that all the world about is illusion. Max Müller sees in the Upanishads of Brahmanism the germs of Buddhism. To his mind there is no break between the India of the Vedas and the India of the Tripitaka—the "Three Baskets" of the Buddhist scriptures.

Desire, in the Buddhist theory, is the ultimate cause of entanglement in the Cycle of Existence, with its miseries and endless rebirth under the Law of Karma, Causation—the one inextricable, indissoluble, inalienable unity of Cause and Effect. The renunciation of desire is the end of unhappiness. ("There is nothing under heaven unto which my heart doth lean," protests Francis Bacon in the "Essay on Death.") To recognize the Four Noble Truths (the "Aryan" Truths)—of misery, its origin, its cessation, and the Path leading to its cessation—and to pursue this Noble Eightfold Path—of right belief, right resolve, right speech, right behavior, right occupation, right effort, right contemplation, right concentration—is to attain *arhat*-ship (sainthood), "the state of him who is worthy," to achieve Nirvana—Cessation—"the dying out"—escape from the round of existence, release from the chain of circumstance; not pessimistic self-annihilation, since the self has no real entity, but the glorious resolution of separateness (to borrow Carlyle's phrase from the *Sartor Resartus*) in the "illimitable ocean of the All." Not lost but at home in the universe.

The dewdrop slips into the shining sea; the spark flies from the forge; the chariot falls apart wanting the charioteer; but while all things pass, man's aim and destiny are real:

"And now, O priests, I take my leave of you," said the Tathagata (the one who has thus come, or thus gone, the Buddha —the Enlightened One), in the farewell to his Order; "all the constituents of being are transitory ["dissolution is the nature of all composite things"]; work out your salvation with diligence."[1]

Buddhism is called a religion without a God, but the Rome, the Mecca, the Zion of Buddhism is Lhasa, Tibet—the Shining Seat, "the Place of God."

Ethical dualism explains the obvious presence of evil in the world but impairs the sovereignty of God. Monism accords God His place but leaves unsolved the "mystery of evil." Job is ready to brave God for an answer. Paul turns the question with a parable.

The most famous dualism is the Mazdean, which aligns the

---

[1] Quoted in Henry Clarke Warren (trans.), *Buddhism in Translations,* p. 109.

world in battle between the two forces of Good and Evil God; but ultimately it too is monism, since after the judgment good alone is left in the universe.

Milton continues the double rulership of the world forever. Satan exults in sight of Paradise.

> Evil be thou my good; by thee at least
> Divided empire with Heaven's King I hold,
> By thee, and more than half perhaps will reign;
> As man ere long, and this new world, shall know.

One of the difficulties of Christian theory is to reconcile the great place given to Christ with God's sole omnipotence. Paul says that when Christ shall have subjected all things to himself, then he too will be subject to God, who has given him the mastery over all things, "that God may be all in all."

The conquests of Alexander brought all religions face to face and invited comparison. The mysticism of India, to which the whole world of sense and existence was Illusion, met the philosophy of Greece, whose quest was Reality—"the things that really are." They sought a common goal: the identity of the real self with God—Atman with Brahman—the individual soul with the soul of the universe. In the introspective phrase of India: "He is my self within the heart" (*Khandogya Upanishad*). "This which rests eternally within the self should be known; and beyond this not anything has to be known" (*Svetasvatara Upanishad*).

The Platonic idealism was found to complement the realistic scheme of Zoroaster. The neo-Platonic idea of the Logos as the mind of God and mediator between God and His world had its equivalent in the Vohu-Mano, the Good Mind, or Good Thought, of the Avesta—the first in the series of the Six Holy Ones, the Amshaspands (the Amesha Spentas)—emanating from the Creator Ahura Mazda and personifying good qualities or Powers in opposition to the corresponding unethical emanations of the Evil Spirit, Ahriman.

The Persian Powers reappear in Philo and are related to God through the mediating Logos. There are six Powers in the allegory of the Ark as representing the world of forms, and the six Leviti-cal cities of refuge on either side Jordan serve for an allegory of higher and lower Powers.

The third in the Persian series of the Six Holy Ones, Good Royalty, appears in Philo as the Royal Power reciprocal with the Creative Power of God. Philo likes the balance of Powers because "Reason is double, both in the universe, and also in the nature of mankind" (*Life of Moses* III.13.1).

The Philonic Powers are not fixed in number, function, or re-lation. They attend on God, are saviors of the world and inter-mediaries in the creation of the higher and immaterial world of ideas. The Powers support the house of the world and the race of men. Again, the Powers are all winged, always eagerly striving for the higher Path leading to the Father. It was not God that came down for Moses and the elders to see but "the presence of His Powers." "Show me thyself," besought Moses. "If not thy glory, then the Powers which attend thee as thy guards."

The cherubim guarding Eden are God's two highest Powers —Sovereignty and Goodness—and the cherubim whose faces turn toward one another and whose wing tips touch over the Mercy Seat in the Holiest Place are the two most ancient and supreme Powers of God—His Creative and His Kingly Power.

The Persians and the Jews had met in the happier day before the Greek came. From the fall of Babylon into the hand of Cyrus until the time of Alexander, Palestine was under Persian domina-tion (539–333 B.C.) The rescript of Cyrus ended the Babylonian Captivity (538/36; "If there was a captivity," says Professor Goodenough) and encouraged the rebuilding of the city and the Temple of Jerusalem. The Isaiah of the Captivity calls Cyrus God's anointed, His shepherd, and loved for Israel's sake. Cyrus' motive may only have been the practical one of settling a loyal people, bound by gratitude, in that seismic country to take the shocks of empire.

There was a real consanguinity of spirit between the Semitic Jew and the Indo-Iranian—the true Aryan—a common ideal of holiness fervently cherished, a purposeful piety to reclaim from death "the living world of righteousness," and an abhorrence of all that is against nature. The *Vendidad* leaves the unnatural sin "unpardoned forever and ever." The sin inexpiable, unatonable, makes of a man a daeva in this life and one of the unseen daevas after death.

Ormadz overcame Ahriman chanting the holiest of all prayers —the Ahuna Vairya. A very free paraphrase runs:

The will of the Lord is the law of righteousness.
The gifts of Vohu-Mano (Good Thought, gatekeeper of Paradise), to the deeds done in this world for Mazda.
He who relieves the poor makes Ahura King.
(*Vendidad* VIII.III.19, p. 100n.)

Contact with the Persians may only have stimulated the growth of a native Jewish angel- and demonology. The Persian eschatology fitted well into the Jewish world scheme. The final conflict, the last judgment, and the resurrection of the dead with the appearance of Saoshyant the Savior at the end of the age— the fourth and last—harmonized with the Jewish messianic prophecies of restoration and judgment.

The Parsi scriptures, preserved by emigrants from Persia to India after the Moslem conquest, cover the whole period of composition of the sacred books of the East.

The metrical hymns, the Gathas, "the victorious, all-healing words" of the Iranian prophet that lifted a people out of darkness into light, are as old as the hymns of the *Rig-Veda* and often reveal a root word in the common Aryan tongue. About 1800 B.C. the tribes left their grazing lands between the Caspian and the Oxus, the eastern branch for the fertile plains of India, the western for the hard, high plateau of Iran, where a man must "labor with the right arm and with the left to do the heavy works of holiness."

The original *Avesta* was written in the hieratic script called the Zend. Properly *Zand* is Pahlavi for *commentary* (the Avesta with its Zand). The primitive Gathas (*ca.* 1800 B.C.)—Zoroaster their last compiler, not their first—form the heart of the Zoroastrian liturgy, the *Yasna.* The *Yashts* (praises), the performance of the *Yasna,* are taken to be younger than the Gathas, and the priestly code, the *Vendidad* (Anti-demonic Law), nineteenth in the original twenty-one Nasks, or books, of the *Avesta,* younger still.

The dating of the *Avesta* ranges from the time Zoroaster committed his revelation to the young Bactrian king Vishtasp, about 600 B.C., to the general completion of the scriptures about the time of the Moslem invasion (*ca.* A.D. 650). James Darmesteter, translator of Parts I and II of the *Avesta* in the *Sacred Books of the East* series, takes the *Vendidad* (volume IV) to contain the oldest laws and the Gathas to be the latest written of the scriptures, the whole existing only in fragments, and recast under the influence of the Bible and Hellenistic Jewish writings in the century before or after Christ.

The translator of the Gathas (*Sacred Books of the East,* vol. XXXI), Lawrence Mills, is sure that the Gathas are in the original vernacular, and no later than 700 B.C., and that the *Vendidad* contains much apocryphal superstition.[2]

At the ancient seat of Bel-Marduk, where most of the Captivity had elected to remain, the Parthian kings extended hospitality to all religions, though they came themselves to be good Zoroastrians. King Valkash (Vologeses I?—about A.D. 50 to 75, contemporary of Nero) ordered a search for all the religious records, written and oral. The Parthians, eastern-most of the Iranians, succeeded the Greek Empire of the Seleucidae (about 250 B.C.) as heirs of the Old Persian Empire of Cyrus and Darius (539–331 B.C.), both men devoted Mazdayasnians.

The Pahlavi version, the present *Avesta,* was compiled by the high priest, Tansar, at the command of the first Sassanian king, founder of the New Persian Empire, Ardashir I (*ca.* A.D. 224–241). Pahlavi derives from Parthian and is a general designation for the Middle Persian dialects. It appears in the inscriptions of Ardashir. The priestly Zend is cognate with the Old Persian found in the cuneiform inscriptions of Cyrus and Darius.

Despite the persecuting zeal of some of the Sassanian kings, the

---

[2] Lawrence Mills, *Our Own Religion in Ancient Persia,* pp. 32–33n.

New Persian line, Babylon remained a world center of religion in Sassanian and even into Moslem times. There eastern and western Asia touched. There Jews and Magi (Zendiks) exerted a mutual influence, reflected in the Babylonian Talmud and, in the opinion of the translator of the Persian scriptures, James Darmesteter, in the *Avesta*. He remarks the rare historic intuition of the Moslems in "assimilating the Zoroastrians to the People of the Book, solving the problem of the origin of the *Avesta*" (K.III.64 ff.).

Then perhaps the Magi needed no star to light their way to Bethlehem.

"If any man preach any other Gospel unto you than that ye have received, let him be accursed." Still, in Paul's own century, in the center from which he evangelized Roman Asia, in the city where the Pauline canon was compiled another gospel was preached. Another wonder-worker, Apollonius of Tyana, came to Ephesus preaching neo-Pythagoreanism.

The earnest desire of the age to know God experientially, to "taste and see that the Lord is good," brought forward the old teachers of religion in a contemporary guise. The new Plato was a blend of Greek philosophy—Plato still, but with a larger admixture of Pythagorean and Orphic mysticism than Plato had known. The new Moses of the mystery is not a strange figure to Philo. Strange to him are the "literalists" who stop at the plain word of Scripture and cannot share his pleasure in the recondite and the obscure implications of allegory (*Fragments,* p. 278).

The old Iranian sun-god Mithra—the Vedic Mitra—was the chief figure in the mystery that overspread the Roman Empire, encouraged by the emperors. Sol Invictus made up a proper equation with Rex Imperator. When Julian determined to revive paganism and crowd out Christianity he became a public votary of Mithras.

A second Persian mystery, Manichaeism, extended its dominion from southern Babylonia, or Persia, the home of Mani's father, a pagan convert to a baptist sect, to central Asia, China, India. Mani drew from all religions and rejected what was distasteful to him. The bitter denunciations of the Christian bishops only prove what a serious rival he was who shared in the fate of their Master, if only in the figurative speech of the Manichaeans describing his persecution by Bahram I and his death in prison (A.D. 276). He claimed to be the Paraclete promised by Christ—a man like himself. But Nicaea had not yet pronounced for the Christian Church. Mani named his predecessors in the sacred office of emissary of the God of Truth as Buddha, Zoroaster, Jesus—not Moses, because he ordained animal sacrifices. Unique among religious founders, who did not generally even write down their own words, Mani illustrated his works with paintings in color.

From Mazdeism came the fruitful figure of the light which served Gnosticism better even than the Jewish prophetic figure of begetting and conceiving. The divinely illuminated soul winged its way along a shaft of light, from sphere to sphere, beyond the sun, to Very Light of Very Light.

On the ground of a common mystic experience, all religions met. Along the path of the mystery Augustine might travel from Mani, to Plato, to Christ.

Whatever the degree of interfusion in the races thus brought together, Alexander's ideal of world unity based on communion of cultures was not an impossible dream. The materials were at hand. A fitting work for the son of Zeus-Amon to tie up the youngest with the oldest civilizations! Eduard Zeller accords Alexander the purest character of all the world conquerors—a character "shaped in strong lines of sagacity, idealism and force" in the words of one biographer, Benjamin Ide Wheeler. Zeller attributes to Aristotle's influence on his youthful pupil the fact that "in spite of later errors, Alexander still stands far above all other world conquerors in nobility of spirit, in purity of morals, in love of humanity, and in personal culture." Aristotle was Alexander's teacher for five or six years preceding his accession to the throne of Macedon in 336 at the age of twenty, but Aristotle had taught him to treat Greeks as friends and barbarians as enemies. Alexander's ten years of conquest had marked a trail of destruction across Asia to India when by the river of Babylon in his thirty-third year the young god lay dead.

HELLENISTIC JUDAISM

A SECOND time the Jew had been invited into Egypt: the first time when "a Syrian ready to perish," "a wandering Aramean"; and now even coerced to colonize the city that was to shine out as a pharos to all the Mediterranean lands. Most prized among the hundreds of thousands of volumes in the libraries of Alexandria, designed to gather the literature of the world, were the books "full of hidden wisdom" that made the Jews desired as faithful citizens. Aristeas, a confidant of Ptolemy II, assures the king that the Jews worship the same God, Zeus, whose name means "life." (Josephus, *Antiquities* XII.II.1 ff.) The Romans continued the privileges allowed the Jews by the Macedonians. They had their own governor, ethnarch, in the two chief cities of the East, Antioch and Alexandria. Philo's brother held the office in Alexandria, where two of the five districts were known as Jewish.

Caligula (A.D. 37–41) interrupted the royal favoritism shown the Jews in the matter of religion. They alone of the peoples of the Empire refused to recognize his pretensions to deity. With the abundant wit that the Jews reserved for idolaters, Philo sketches the progress of Caius' madness: his appearance at first in the character and costume of the half-gods, Bacchus, Hercules, and the twins Castor and Pollux; and then his assumption of full deity in the persons of the gods Mercury, Apollo, Mars; last as sole deity, ordering a colossal statue with the title Jupiter to be set up in the very Sanctum Sanctorum of the Jerusalem Temple.

"Did you imitate the beneficent works of these gods? Or did you wish to be an immortal only to have your infamies perpetuated? Is there no god worthy even of a small precinct?" asks Philo.

Even the worldly-minded Agrippa, hearing from the lips of his royal benefactor of the intended impiety, passes into a swoon that lasts two days. He wakes and addresses a memorial to Caius. No one had ventured to violate the sanctity of the Temple. Augustus had vowed a perpetual daily burnt offering that was still being presented at the Temple where Caius' maternal grandfather, M. Agrippa, had entered only to admire and adore.

The Jewish ethnic tale is interwoven with the Egyptian and the Greek. Josephus counts out the seventy names of Jacob's family, difficult as they are to Greek readers, only to answer those who say that the Jews came from Egypt, not originally from Mesopotamia. Gladly would the Egyptians claim Moses for their own, acknowledging him to be a wonderful and a divine person. He conducted the successful Egyptian war against Ethiopia (Cush) and married the Ethiopian king's daughter, Tharbis, who had fallen in love with him (Num. 12:1; Josephus, *Ant.* II.10).

Manetho (*ca.* 250 B.C.), the priestly compiler of the Egyptian dynasties, calls the Jewish lawgiver a priest, by birth of Heliopolis, named Osarsiph (from Osiris, one of the ennead of Heliopolis, god of the mysteries), who changed to his true name, Moses— Moüses—"drawn out" (of the water).

Another writer, Cheremon, calls Moses and Joseph scribes, Joseph a sacred scribe, and gives their original Egyptian names as Tesithen and Peteseph. The name that Pharaoh gave Joseph means "the god speaks and he lives," and Asenath, Joseph's Egyptian wife, daughter of the priest of On, is "the favorite of the goddess Neith." (Josephus, *Apion* book I, 28–32.)

Moses is related to the Greek myth through Musaeus, father of Orpheus, god of the mysteries, and the near progeny of Abraham is associated with Hercules. Hercules married the daughter of a son of Keturah, Abraham's third wife, in appreciation of aid against Antaeus and the Libyans. The third marriage of Abraham explains remoter relationships as Hagar explains the Semitic cousin, the desert Arab.

The Greeks were not without curiosity on the subject of the

Jews. One of the Peripatetics, Clearchus, is cited by Josephus against Apion. Aristotle was praising a certain Syrian Jew, his strict continence in diet, and his habits of life. "These Jews are derived from the Indian philosophers," Josephus quotes Aristotle as saying to Clearchus. "They are named by the Indians Calami, and by the Syrians Sudaei and took their name from the country they inhabit, which is called Judea; but for the name of their city it is a very awkward one, for they call it Jerusalem." (Hierosolyma or Hierousalem.)

Clearchus spoke of the Jews only by way of digression; but another philosopher, Hecateus of Abdera, wrote a whole book on the Jews. The "father of history," Herodotus of Halicarnassus, knew them by the tribal rite; and the "father of philosophy," "the superior of all the philosophers in wisdom and piety towards God, Pythagoras of Samos, not only knew the Jewish doctrines but in great measure admired and followed them."

The story that Josephus tells of Alexander's visit to Jerusalem after the conquest of Gaza may be such a Hellenizing legend. Alexander approached unattended to pay homage to the high priest, who came out to welcome him in the robes of office at the head of a procession of habited priests and a multitude in white, and knelt to adore the Name on the high priest's mitre. Such an one had come to Alexander in a dream to announce that he would be the conqueror of the Persian Empire.

Most especially in the mystery which came from the East do the Greeks and Romans find correspondences with the Jews. The lulab is the thyrsus to the Hellenists. Plutarch hears the cry of the mystic devotees, "(Euoi) Saboi," in the Jewish Shabat, the Sabbath; and the Feast of Tabernacles, coming at the vintage season, is in worship of Dionysus.

The Roman Tacitus does not see a festival of the jovial Bacchus, conqueror of the East, in the Jewish Succoth; but the Sabbatic year honors Saturn, who was banished from Crete with the Idaeans, the fathers of this Jewish race. The likeness in sound between Judaei and Idaei leads Tacitus to link the Jews with the homeland of the first great age of Aegean culture.

Pliny the Elder records that Dionysus settled Scythopolis in Palestine, the biblical Beth-shean, to protect the tomb of his nurse.

The Greek historians have not thought Moses worthy of mention, writes Philo, beginning the *Life of Moses,* but neither have they recorded the virtuous and praiseworthy of their own race. Philo exalts both races to the stars. The souls of the Jews were brought forth by divine agency, making them nearly related to God, but the Greek intellect is supreme: "For Greece is the only country which really produces man, that heavenly plant, that divine offshoot, producing that most accurately refined reason which is appropriated by and akin to knowledge." (Philo IV, p. 240.)

Socrates is an example of the power of virtue:

Do we then now wonder if Socrates, and such and such a virtuous man, has lived in purity? men who have never once studied any of the means of providing themselves with pecuniary resources, and who have never, even when it was in their power, condescended to accept great gifts which have been tendered to their acceptance by wealthy friends or mighty kings, because they looked upon the acquisition of virtue as the only good, the only beautiful thing, and have therefore labored at that, and disregarded all other good things. (Philo IV, p. 227; found in Eusebius, *Preparation of the Gospel,* book VIII.13)

But Moses is "the greatest and most perfect man that ever lived . . . for the glory of the laws which he left behind him has reached over the whole world, and has penetrated to the very furthest reaches of the universe." "In accordance with the providential will of God he was both a king and a lawgiver, and a high priest and a prophet," displaying the most eminent wisdom and virtue in each of his four powers (*Life of Moses* I.1; II.1).

The Jews did not live on the world's highway, in the path of successive world empires, and remain as oblivious to the march of ideas as they were made painfully aware of the march of armies. Josephus, Philo, the Maccabees, bear ample testimony to the appeal of Hellenic thought. The blow struck by Mattathias, inaugurating the revolt under the Maccabees, was as much a protest against the seductive power of Hellenism as against the tyranny of Antiochus.

The Jews who broke the law of the Central Sanctuary and built a great temple on the exact model of the one at Jerusalem, instead of a humble meeting place for the reading of the Law, at Leontopolis, in "the Nome of the Cat," and another such "altar to the Lord in the midst of the land of Egypt" (Isa. 19:19) at the First Cataract in the island of Elephantine, which Cambyses spared when he overthrew the temples of the natives gods . . . the Jews who lined the walls of their synagogues with frescoes depicting Bible scenes in mystic Philonic allegories like those unearthed at Dura, in the region of the ancient capital Mari on the middle Euphrates . . . were liberated from a narrow tradition.

The last compiler of the Sirach, in the second prologue, complains that the Hebrew words lose force in the Greek, not blaming his own deficiency in Hebrew. The Jews who read the Old Testament in Greek because they were unable to read it in Hebrew would not falter at Greek terms like *Logos,* for the word from Heaven, at *mystery* for the divine revelation, at adding their oracles to the pagan Sibyl's.

Luke speaks of Greeks and Hellenists, the Greek Jews (cf. Acts 6:1; 9:29; 14:1; and 11:20, Greeks, or Hellenists). Between the "Hebrews" and the "Hellenists" stood Paul, distrusted by the conservatives, disputed by the liberals.

The local Hebrew meetinghouse where subtile points of law were interminably argued with the preciseness of the Sophists, resembled the philosopher's school of the Greeks, whose intellectual curiosity took them even to the synagogue.

Even to this day, the Jews hold philosophic discussions on the seventh day, disputing about their national philosophy and devoting that day to the knowledge and consideration of the subjects of natural philosophy; for as for their houses of prayer in the different cities, what are they, but schools of wisdom, and courage, and temperance, and justice, and piety and holiness and every virtue by which human and divine things are appreciated, and placed upon a proper footing? (*Life of Moses,* III.27.4)

No Holy Writ derives from the Greek oracles. Even the Delphic "Nothing overmuch" and "Know thyself" ("Know that thou art but a man") are adopted from the Seven Sages. Our knowledge of the religion of the Greeks comes from secular poets, orators, philosophers, and the remains of Greek art.

The one prophetic voice in Greek literature is Hesiod's sober cry for justice under Heaven, and if Homer loves the deeds of chivalry, disclaiming the plebeian tales of the elder world, Hesiod's heart is with the toiling poor. The *Works and Days* and the *Theogony* tell of the origin of evil in a woman's seductiveness—"that sheer delusion unescapable for men." *Works and Days* traces the ages of the world from the first golden race of men, of one seed with the gods, to the present degenerated race of iron, reckless of the oath (*horkos*) for whose violation even gods do long penance.

The *Theogony* gives the complex line of gods from the beginning, the order of creation—first Chaos . . . Darkness and Night . . . Bright Sky (Ether) and Day . . . and then broadbosomed Earth (Ge, Gaia) bore Heaven to be like herself an eternal abode of the blessed gods. Earth bore Sea (Pontos) and, in union with Heaven (Uranos), deep-eddying Okeanos and lovely Tethys among the twelve Titans. Kronos is the youngest of the sons. Dread Styx, daughter of Ocean and Tethys, the first to enlist in aid of Zeus against the Titans, is honored as "the mighty oath of the gods."

For the dim figure of the Titan the mind substitutes Time (Chronos). Zeus, "Father of gods and men," supplanter of the elder line, is truly child of Time. At Earth's importunity, Kronos had sundered his mother from his hated sire's too close embrace, and from the severed member of Uranos cast into the sea, the waves returned the foam-born Aphrodite, "Queen of Smiles, Lady of Laughter," and in her wake Love (Eros) and fair Desire, for the power of love is "the fairest among the deathless gods."

Homer introduces us to "the aristocrats of Olympus," as Moore terms them. The Ionian poet is the incarnation of the happy Greek soul. He is not overreverent toward the gods. His men are better than his gods and his gods are only men. Zeus, "Father of gods and men," rules a turbulent family. The gods are immediately concerned in the affairs of men, and partisanship on their behalf divides the House of Heaven.

Plato's doctrine of the Ideas merely revives Homer's old gods, in Walter Pater's opinion,[1] and Plato's doctrine of creation is only ancient Hesiod to Philo:

> First verily was created Chaos,
> Then broad-breasted Earth appeared.

He remarks that some persons consider Hesiod to be the father of Platonic thought.

The idealist Plato builds on the realist ethic of his teacher Socrates. The universal definitions, the generalized concepts of Socrates, became, in the mystic genius of Plato, living, divine beings, prototypes of earthly things partaking of the nature of the Absolute and the Eternal. The large genius of Plato fed two streams: the mysticism of the neo-Platonists and the scientific abstractions of the master of logic, Aristotle. *Ipse dixit* ("Himself said") terminated any scholastic argument.

The "realism" of the Schoolmen is Platonic "idealism," and their "nominalism" is in effect Aristotelian— our "realism." Transubstantiation is a realist doctrine defended on the Aristotelian ground of a distinction between essential substance and accidental attributes (*On Categories,* chapter 5). The early Middle Ages knew Aristotle only from two of his six logical works—the treatises *On Definitions* and *On Categories*—and did not perceive the difference between the two masters, which was mainly in the point of departure in inquiry—Plato from the ideal and the eternal, Aristotle from the actual, material, phenomenal world.

The inexorable logic of action in the dramatic poets constitutes a moral unity, marred by the conflict of the Powers that govern life. "Character is Destiny." Fate is God—a retributive rather than a redeeming God. Orestes, having obeyed the voice

---

[1] Walter Pater, *Plato and Platonism,* p. 168.

of Apollo, who speaks no prophetic word except it be from his father Zeus, and avenged his father's death on his mother, is pursued by the Furies (Conscience) even to madness.

The "king of men," Agamemnon, dreading to disobey the priest Calchas, who has always spoken truth, brings down wrath on all his house because he sacrifices his daughter Iphigenia to speed the holy war against Troy.

The high-souled Oedipus, sinning in ignorance, is destroyed by remorse; and a blind wanderer in the Forest of the Furies is at last granted release without hope, except the vague grace of a death in which he is favored of Heaven.

The divine hero Hercules leaves his son in the dilemma of obeying his filial oath, exacted under threat of the curse of Heaven, and disobeying the divine law in marrying her who has been the cause of both his mother's and his father's death. The son berates the gods who can witness such sufferings unashamed, though themselves called fathers—

> Sufferings many and strange indeed,
> And none of them, save what Zeus decreed.

Even the pious Hesiod is said to have been betrayed to an unworthy death by the Delphic oracle—in one story when he came to present the fruits of victory over Homer to the god. The king had awarded the honors to Hesiod against popular clamor because "he taught peace and agriculture, and not war and slaughter like Homer." The oracle hails Hesiod with these ambiguous words:

Happy is this man who visiteth my house, even Hesiod, honored of the deathless Muses: his glory shall be wide-flung as the dawn. But beware thou of the fair grove of Nemean Zeus: for there the end of death is foredoomed for thee. (Hesiod, Intro., pp. xxv, xxx).

In all his trials—trials, not betrayals—righteous Job has one unconquerable conviction: his Redeemer lives.

The city built by Alexander at the natural confluence of three continents had in its greatest days no rivals except Rome and Antioch. Before its founding Alexander had effectuated prophecy in sinking the Queen of Trade in the midst of the seas, and later Rome was to find it expedient to delete Carthage, the too-thriving daughter city of Tyre, from the map.

Alexandria, with its university, the museum, and the famous libraries, was the location chosen by the Septuagint translators of the Bible in the middle of the third century B.C. for its properly salubrious spiritual climate, as Josephus tells the story. Here in the land that had always been open to the settler, the trader, the wanderer, Alexander's dream was most completely realized. Here took place as free an interchange in ideas as in the goods gotten from the ends of the earth.

The Alexandrine Philo Judaeus (*ca.* 20 B.C.—*ca.* A.D. 50), Greek philosopher and good Jew, attempted to create a universally acceptable harmony of Hebrew supernaturalism and Greek rationalism, to make all the philosophers and poets of Greece sing the "new song" of redemption.

"That part of a man's religion which is convenient he will never forget," says Trader Horn, and no method of exegesis is so convenient as allegory: perhaps none is so true to the sense of a primitive, metaphorical language in which inspiration speaks in figures and parables meant for him that is able to hear.

Stories like the sacrifice of Isaac and Iphigenia had offended the sensibilities of a much earlier day than Philo's, and a substitute victim had been provided. The sacrifice of Jephthah's daughter in Judges is the primitive tale that, somehow, escaped editorial scrutiny. Jephthah's daughter was the virgin sacrifice like Iphigenia, who, deceitfully decked for her bridals with Achilles, was slain by her father at the altar. Only in the story of a later day was she snatched up from the altar by the Goddess of Virgins, Artemis, who left a deer for offering in her stead.

Because we must by all means consider the Holy Scriptures infallible, Philo defends Rebecca's duplicity in the matter of Esau's birthright. Rebecca is admired as patience and Jacob is the man perfect in soul who has destroyed the roughnesses of passions and vices. Philo's simple and pure philosophic soul, accepting the literal word of Scripture, delights in the spiritual interpretation. He would not pass by any allegorical meaning concealed beneath the plain language "from that natural love of more recondite and laborious knowledge which is accustomed to seek for what is obscure before, and in preference to, what is evident" (*On Ten Commandments,* 1.1).

The twelfth-century Maimonides counsels the student to acquire first a knowledge of the figures in the understanding of the Prophets, next of the general ideas, then the meaning of each word: but he must not search for deep meanings in the details of every allegory. The Parable of the Strange Woman is only a lesson in continence (*Guide for the Perplexed,* Intro. pp. 5-8).

The parabolic meaning is like apples of gold in vessels of silver filigree for the keen-sighted to discern. In every word with a double intent, the plain literal meaning is silver—useful wisdom—but the profound, hidden meaning is gold—the Hesperian fruit, the Edenic pomegranate, the delectable treasure.

Philo expounds the sacrifice of Isaac: "The mind, when it is rendered perfect, will pay its proper tribute to the God who causes perfection. For then it will sacrifice its beloved son, not a man (for the wise man is not a slayer of his children), but the male offspring of a virtuously living soul, the fruit which germinates from it"—and a mystery to the soul that bore it. (*On the Migration of Abraham* 25.1.)

Hagar's flight was Abram himself led astray by earthly learning, the accessory, the natural handmaid of virtue, the liaison with Hagar motivated only by the desire for offspring. Sarah's cruelty was the reclamation to virtue, the wise man's true spouse, by whom he can now beget spiritual offspring. The Lord God appeared to Abram in His double power, in His creative attribute as God and in His royal attribute as Lord, and told Abram that his name was to be changed to Abraham, "the father of many nations"—as a father endowed with the power and authority to rule the nations (the multifarious inclinations of the will).

"These passions are the causes of all good, and of all evil:

of good when they submit to the authority of dominant reason, and of evil when they break out of bounds and scorn all government and restraint" (*Life of Moses,* I.6).

Abraham, the father of the Jewish race, is one of those heroes of peace who go unarmed.

> There were the giants famous from the beginning, that were of so great stature, and so expert in war. Those did not the Lord choose, neither gave he the way of knowledge unto them:
> But they were destroyed, because they had no wisdom, and perished through their own foolishness. (Baruch 3:26–28)

The mastodon perished and man lived. And mastodon-man will perish.

The Philonic type and symbol we meet again in Paul—the inevitable method whereby the simple is intellectualized. Paul turns to his purpose the Scripture on the Law in the mouth and the heart of man. The literal proscription on muzzling the ox that treads the corn Paul removes to the spiritual domain. Paul has a Philonic construction on Hagar and Sarah.

In the same mode the rabbi writes his supercommentary on the Law:

> "When thou walkest it shall lead thee"—in this world. "When thou liest down it shall watch over thee"—in the grave. "When thou wakest it shall talk with thee"—in the world to come. (Pirke Aboth [Chapters of the Fathers] 6:10)

And Philo's brother Platonist, Augustine, reads deep purposes of the divine grace into the simple Bible narrative by the method of allegory. Moses "when by revelation of the Spirit he saith, 'In the beginning God created heaven and earth,'" signifies by *heaven* "that spiritual or intellectual creature which always beholds the face of God," and by the earth "'invisible and without form' the corporeal creature. . . . 'Let there be light, and there was light,' I understand of the spiritual creature; because there was already a sort of life which Thou mightest illuminate." "Thy spirit was 'borne above' the waters" (the unchangeable supereminence of Divinity above all things changeable)—above "the darkness of ignorance" which cloaked unregenerated creation.

"'Thy mercy forsook not our misery, and Thou saidst, 'Let there be light.' 'Repent ye, for the kingdom of heaven is at hand. Repent ye, let there be light.'. . . And our darkness displeased us, we turned unto Thee, and there was light."

Augustine offers a valid defense of his method: "Why may not Moses mean what we all mean?—So great a man, God's faithful servant in those books . . . which for so long after were to profit all nations, and through the whole world, from such an eminence of authority, were to surmount all sayings of false and proud teachings." (*Confessions,* Books XII, XIII.)

How could the Pharisaic Jew have fallen into his soteriological refrain "Our Lord and Savior Jesus Christ" and in his most ardent Jewish "blessings" collocated that name with the Name of the Father?

The character of Moses in the apocryphal Assumption of Moses wants little to make an avatar. Barth defines the true avatar: "The presence, at once mystic and real, of the Supreme Being in a human individual, who is both truly God and truly man, and this intimate union of the two natures is conceived of as surviving the death of the individual in whom it was realized." (Barth, *Religions of India,* p. 170.)

Joshua calls Moses "my lord Moses." He is "Lord of the Word" in the Assumption. The Word (Logos) is more potent than was ever spoken through a prophet or inculcated precept upon precept, line upon line. It has power to slay; it did slay the host of the Egyptians: and power to save, as Aaron stayed the destruction in the wilderness through the potency of the Word in the symbolic dress of the high priest.

For in the long garment was the whole world, and in the four rows of the stones was the glory of the fathers graven, and Thy Majesy upon the diadem of his head. (Wisdom of Solomon 18:24)

For the law designs that he should be the partaker of a nature superior to that of man; inasmuch as he approaches more nearly to that of the Deity; being, if one must say the plain truth, on the borders between the two, in order that men may propitiate God by some mediator, and that God may have some subordinate

minister by whom he may offer and give his mercies and kind-
nesses to mankind. (Philo, *On Monarchy*, II.12.3)

Moses was foreordained and prepared before the foundation
of the world to be the mediator of God's convenant, and in the
next world intercessor for sin. He is "the sacred spirit who was
worthy of the Lord, manifold and incomprehensible, the Lord of
the Word, who was faithful in all things, God's chief prophet
throughout the earth, the most perfect teacher in the world."[2]
The very title of the apocalypse of Moses—Assumption—implies
a divine existence, since he passes without death. Josephus implies
that same order of being: "Moses wrote in the holy books that
he died for fear that they should say that for his virtue he went
to God" (*Antiquities* IV.8.48).

The accusation against Stephen in Acts collocates Moses with
God: "We have heard him speak blasphemous words against
Moses, and against God."

The wisdom for which Solomon labored in Ecclesiastes, which
may be achieved by rigorous training, comes as the reward of
prayer in the later wisdom writings, as a mystic marriage with the
heavenly spouse Wisdom.

"There is no Royal Road to geometry," says Euclid to the
first Ptolemy, who asks an easier way than his *Elements.* There
is no immediate divine illumination in this subject: there is no
light-stream pouring down from on high.

The metaphysical does not crowd out the messianic dream.
Josephus tells the story of the royal wastrel, Herod Agrippa I,
receiving the promise of a large loan from Philo's brother, ala-
barch or ethnarch of Egypt, given in admiration of his wife's,
Cypros', loyalty, or for a deeper motive—that this amiable prince
answered the promise of Isaiah. ("Who is this that cometh from
Edom?"—63:1.)

When Agrippa became king he kept the ritual law most meticu-
lously and every day offered the appropriate sacrifice. He chose

---

2 Assumption of Moses 11:16–17.

the occasion of a celebration in honor of Claudius to inaugurate his messianic role, appearing in the theater clothed in silver that blazed in the morning sun, drawing the acclamation "Not a man but a god!" Agrippa, looking up, saw the ominous owl, the owl that had presaged good to him when a prisoner at Rome, and he knew that the curse of "Herod's evil" was upon him. It was God's reproof. He could only resign himself to the will of God and give thanks for the happiness that he had enjoyed. ("The Lord gave and the Lord hath taken away: Blessed be the Name of the Lord.")

Did Philo, when he came up to Jerusalem to offer prayer and sacrifice, ever pass his youthful contemporary of Galilee discoursing to his devoted poor in the porch of the Temple? And though Philo knew the equality of all souls before God and believed that a wise man's soul outweighs the world, did he ever pause to hear? And yet the youth was candidate for the same honor as Agrippa, claimant for the one crown. And the wise men of the East and the lovers of wisdom from the West came to pay him homage as their King.

Emerson makes an entry in his journal on "a youth who owed nothing to fortune and who was 'hanged at Tyburn.'" Yet the youth who "owed nothing to fortune" had a wonderful father and a lovely mother. He was heir to one thousand years of prophecy. He had only to take up the stuff of the parables and the discourses, add the magic of his own personality, and there they are the perfection of art—"a familiar thing become divine i' the utterance!" The youth who owed nothing to fortune came at the central point of human history, to the geographic center of the world, then as now. The stage was prepared for him as for that other fortune's favorite, Alexander; and the crowning death, when the future seemed fairest, only added to their fame.

Agrippa's ambition resulted in tumult and death. Jesus resolutely rejected any political aims:

"My kingdom is not of this world.". . .
"Art thou a king then?". . .
"Thou sayest that I am a king."

THE LIVING GOD

THE vital questions of man's nature, his relationship to God, and his obligation to his fellow men were discussed in every school in the world. A teacher and his disciples constituted a school, and these discussions were their meat and drink. John expresses the ardor of the Christian disciples: "Evermore give us this bread." If the *Rubáiyát* is a Sufi love poem, and God is the Sufi's love, the invitation to the Beloved to fill the cup must refer to the wine of life: whoso drinks of it shall never thirst again. "Brimful of sweet wine," they said of the disciples at Pentecost. No, says Peter; drunk with the Spirit of God!

The answers to the questions show the variations of racial temperament and individual intuition. Frequently the difference is only in emphasis. Often there is remarkable unanimity.

Paul and Mencius, a world apart in their premise on man's essential nature—Mencius, whose spiritual pride contrasts sharply with the humility of the Master, more assured than Confucius of man's innate virtue: Paul convinced that as in Adam all have sinned and died, so only in Christ shall they live—still agree in their practical conclusion.

"For he that soweth to his flesh," Paul warns the Galatians, "shall of the flesh reap corruption; but he that soweth to the Spirit shall of the Spirit reap life everlasting." (6:8.)

"The disciple Kung-tu said, 'All are equally men, but some are great men, and some are little men;—how is this?' Mencius replied, 'Those who follow that part of themselves which is great are great men; those who follow that part which is little are little men. . . . Let a man first stand fast in the supremacy of the nobler part of his constitution, and the inferior part will not be able to take it from him. It is simply this which makes the great man' " (Mencius, book VI, part I, chapter 15).

Weymouth's New Testament in Modern Speech brings Paul even nearer to Mencius: "He who sows in the field of his lower nature, will from that nature reap destruction; but he who sows to serve the Spirit [the human spirit?] will from the Spirit reap the Life of the Ages" (Gal. 6:8).

Another prolific source of argument—the freedom of the will—draws from the saint the despairing cry, "For I know that in me [that is, in my flesh] dwelleth no good thing: for to will is present with me; but how to perform that which is good I find not. For the good that I would, I do not: but the evil which I would not, that I do": but from the sage the confident assertion, "The will is the leader of the passion-nature. The passion-nature pervades and animates the body. The will is first and chief, and the passion-nature is subordinate to it."[1]

The modern psychologist William James agrees with Mencius: "However weak the will, the side on which it is thrown always triumphs."

It may be asked why people should have subjected themselves to the hard disciplines of ancient religion, assuming that the priests were the authors of the ancient laws. But both Moses and Ezra read the Law to the people and received their assent. Only then was the covenant sealed. Without the acquiescence of the people the priests could never have enforced religious observances with the penalties for every breach of Law.

The modern mind is struck most in ancient religion by the often moderate punishment for an obvious crime and the fearful penalty for a cultic offense: but for material breaches of the law the consequences are apparent, while cultic offenses disturb the spiritual order with results that cannot be apprehended.

The Persian slaying a beneficent animal whose business in life is to destroy the noxious creations of the Evil Spirit, or performing rites of purification without knowing the law of Mazda,

---

[1] James Legge (trans.), *The Chinese Classics,* vol. II: *The Works of Mencius,* book II, part I, chapter 2:9.

and the Jew breaking the Sabbath or the rules of personal or ritual purity, infringe on world order; and each member of the religious community must absolve himself from any guilty participation, however near the offender, and so avert impending disaster (Deut. 13).

Why, then, did people take to their hearts and retain, long after the original meaning was lost and the mind had outgrown them, beliefs and practices from which they suffered so much? They did not make an offering to their God of that which cost them nothing. The answer is plain: because they once found God in those things. The constant and unifying principle is the belief in God—from magic formulae to mystic contemplations— God.

*   *   *

The Master being very sick, Tsze-lu asked leave to pray for him. He said, "May such a thing be done?" Tsze-lu replied, "It may. In the Eulogies it is said, 'Prayer has been made for thee to the spirits of the upper and lower worlds.' " The Master said, "My praying has been for a long time." (*Analects of Confucius* VII.34)

To the great revealers of man's religious nature to himself, there was nothing supernatural in direct communion with God; rather was it supremely natural. They invited all to share in the divine beneficence.

Mohammed called prayer the pillar of religion and the key of Paradise; there could be no good in a religion without prayer. Every Moslem land answers the muezzin's call to prayer:

God is most great.
I testify that there is no God but God.
I testify that Muhammad is the Apostle of God.
Come to prayer.
Come to salvation.
Prayer is better than sleep. (*In the first morning call.*)
God is most great.
There is no God but God. (Hughes, *Dictionary of Islam*)

The Shi'ahs insert in the Azan "Come to the best of works."

With this work the Hebrew Psalmist identifies himself completely: "I [am] prayer." (*"Ani tefillah."*)

Mohammed rejected both trumpet and bell in favor of the human voice to sound the call to prayer. Hughes, in the *Dictionary of Islam* (p. 28), quotes the accounts of old travelers who record the Azan as a tuneless cry in Bokhara, for it is sinful to add artifice in religion; in Cairo, a harmony of loud, sonorous voices was most impressive on the stillness of the night; and the plaintive melancholy "announcement" which floated over the Bosphorus from Istanbul at the fall of day was an appealing reminder that God is most great and that there is no God but God.

> *Allahu akbar . . .*
> *la ilaha illa (A)Llah.*

* * *

Always the religious teacher speaks the infinite Word of God. "Unroll it and it fills the universe; roll it up, and it retires and lies hid in mysteriousness" (*Tao*). The secret doctrine of Brahman is "worth more than the whole sea-girt earth full of treasure." The Word outweighs the world.

The rabbi comments on the Torah: "Turn it and turn it again, for the whole is in it, and the whole of thee is in it, and from it swerve not, for there is to thee no greater good than it." Moses is "the Lord of the Word." (Pirke Aboth 5:25.)

Zoroaster, like the Hebrew prophets, learned the doctrine in direct converse with the Almighty. Even the natural ethic of Socrates obeys the sign from Heaven and is inspired by the divine voice. "And who erreth more widely from the truth than he who followeth his own desire without a direction from God?" (K. XXVIII.51.)

These religious teachers are not conscious reformers. They reaffirm the old foundations. Confucius calls himself "a transmitter and not a maker [or creator], believing in and loving the ancients." Buddha was evidently not founding a religion when he excluded women from his order. Moses spoke in the name of the God of the Fathers, and Jesus repudiated the intention of abrogating the least provision of the Law.

So easily does the Divine Word flow from what has gone before: so unobtrusively does it appear among men.

Kipling tells a legend of the tribesman who possessed "the magic of the necessary word." When others were struck dumb, his words "became alive and walked up and down in the hearts of all his hearers." In dread of his magic power the tribe killed the man; then they saw that the magic was in the words, not in the man.[2]

There are words in the Bible that must always have been magic—words of enchantment. But the word that is preserved becomes the sacred word. Some flame like beacons on a mountain-top: some gleam like fireflies out of the dark: and some are gad-flies—they only sting.

"Take with you words and turn to the Lord."

The Sanskrit term for the divine revelation is *shrutih—shruti,* "the hearing." The insistent plea of the Bible is that men hear. The woman blesses the mother of Jesus: "Yea, rather, blessed are they that hear the word of God and keep it." Jesus asks that he be heard, even though he be not believed. He does not condemn unbelief, but the word that he has spoken that condemns. Truth is self-authenticating: otherwise it would require the witness of the lie.

The Jewish Gnosticism of the Kabbala identifies the Divine Word with the voice of the Living God, producing all forms of beings. The Word with God at the creation, himself God, is that divine voice that sounded over the primeval waste of waters before the formation of the world. The first creative act of God is the "Word."

"As far as Brahman reaches, so far reaches speech:—wherever there is Brahman, there is a word; and wherever there is a word, there is Brahman." (*Upanishads.*)

Job wished that his words might be inscribed in a book and engraved with a pen of iron in the rock forever.

Shelley wrote of the poet and his dream:

---

2 Rudyard Kipling, *A Book of Words.*

... Create he can
Forms more real than living Man,
Nurselings of immortality!

By what extension of term, by what metaphorical process, does the living word of Scripture, the word in the mouth and in the heart of man, the very voice of God, the word of faith, become the Word incarnate and the Creating God? What outward propulsion is needed?

Drummond in the *Philo* turns every fragment of Greek philosophy for some hint on the Logos. He sees none in Plato. As far back as the Ionian, Heraclitus of Ephesus (500 B.C.), he finds: "Of this Logos existing always men are without understanding"; and "All things happen according to this Logos." Drummond sees the law of the cosmic Logos in the quaint poetics of Fragment 29: "The sun will not transgress its measures; but if so the Erinyes, the defenders of right, will find it out": "The Logos is not yet the Word because there is no transcendent God whose word it could be." (Pp. 32, 46.)

The doctrine of primal soul belongs to Heraclitus. The soul is fire, and the Logos is fire, and the first principle of the universe is soul.

I Am that which began;
Out of me the years roll;
Out of me God and man;
I am equal and Whole;
God changes and man, and the form of
them bodily. I am the soul.

More familiar, perhaps, than Swinburne's expression is Tennyson's "Hymn to the Logos" in the invocation to the *In Memoriam*:

Strong Son of God, immortal Love,
    Whom we, that have not seen thy face,
    By faith, and faith alone, embrace,
Believing where we cannot prove;

Thine are these orbs of light and shade;
    Thou madest Life in man and brute;
    Thou madest Death; and lo, thy foot
Is on the skull which thou hast made.

Thou wilt not leave us in the dust:
  Thou madest man, he knows not why,
  He thinks he was not made to die;
And thou hast made him: thou art just.

Thou seemest human and divine,
  The highest, holiest manhood, thou.
  Our wills are ours, we know not how;
Our wills are ours, to make them thine.

Our little systems have their day;
  They have their day and cease to be;
  They are but broken lights of thee,
And thou, O Lord, art more than they.

There is a possible hint on the Word in the logion of Isaiah 52:6 (cf. Douay version): "Therefore my people shall know my name in that day: for I myself that spoke, behold I am here." (An existence in the Word and apart from the Word.)

Just as tenuous a hint occurs in the ancient text of the Passover Haggadah: "And I shall pass through the Land of Egypt. I am not an angel. I am not a seraph. I am in the Word."

Philo expounds the Word which he takes to be spoken by God in His own person, "In the image of God I made man":

No mortal thing could have been formed on the Similitude of the supreme Father of the universe, but only after the pattern of the second deity, who is the Word of the Supreme Being; since it is fitting that the rational soul of man should bear before it the type of the Divine Word; since in His first Word God is superior to the most rational possible nature. (*Questions in Genesis* II.62, on Gen. 9:6)

Created man was made of dust and earth, formed as a vessel by the hand of the potter, a mixture of corruptible and incorruptible, of body and soul: of senses and passions of the blood. But the man made in the image of God—made in the image of the Word of God—never inhabited the world of sense. He is invisible, incorporeal, intellectual.

One more glance at Philo's Logos: "This is the Word of God, the first beginning of all things, the original species or archetypal idea, the first measure of the universe" (*Questions in Exodus* 1:4; cf. Eph. 4:13).

And created man is "a kind of copy of the Powers of God, a visible image of an invisible nature, a created image of an uncreated and immortal original" (*Life of Moses* II.12).

Philo complains that the polytheists have "cut away the most beautiful support of the soul, namely, the proper conception of the ever-living God" (*On Ten Commandments* XIV.3).

The Jews said that theirs was the true Living God. Everything about Him lived. Living beings supported His throne. His word was a living word. His way was ever new and living.

But the "awful race of the gods is deathless"—the daemons, the Powers whose worship Paul denounces as opposed to the worship of God.

"Those that are attached to the Living God do all live," Philo renders Deuteronomy 4:4.

"Therefore we both labor and suffer reproach because we trust in the Living God who is the Savior of all men, especially of those that believe" (I Tim. 4:10).

The author of Ephesians reminds his Gentile constituency that once they were alien from the commonwealth of Israel, and ignorant of the "covenants of promise," "having no hope and without God in the world" (2:12).

The Unmovable Mover of Aristotle, to whom man is naturally attracted, is not gracious to man. But how know God if He refuses to know you? For religion is communion. Not only must you acknowledge your God, but your God must acknowledge you. Paul is amazed that the Galatians can return to the rudimentary notions from which they were delivered after they "have known God, or rather are known of God" (4:9).

The Chinese sage, lamenting that no one knows him, comforts himself: "But there is Heaven;—that knows me!" (*Analects* XIV.37.)

Philo objects to the animal worship of Egypt, which the Egyptians kept, to the amusement of the ancient world:

Therefore God, removing out of his sacred legislation all such impious deification of undeserving objects, has invited men to the honor of the one true and living God; not indeed that he has any need himself to be honored; for being all-sufficient for himself, he has no need of anyone else; but he has done so, because he wished to lead the race of mankind, hitherto wandering about in trackless deserts, into a road from which they should not stray, that so by following nature it might find the best end of all things, namely, the knowledge of the true and living God, who is the first and most perfect of all good things; from whom, as from a fountain, all particular blessings are showered upon the world, and upon the things and people in it. (*On Ten Commandments* 16.4)

To compare the Living God with the gods that never lived, with the idols that terrify no more than a scarecrow in a cucumber patch, was a prime satiric theme. But the Jews came to make idols of the Law, the Temple, the Sabbath, and when Jesus reaffirmed the root concept of Judaism, the sacredness of personality that the Sabbath and the laws of blood were meant to enforce, he was guilty of sacrilege. An image does not constitute an idol: idolatry is a thing of the mind. *"Thou shalt not make unto thee a graven image."* The Psalmist recalls the reproach of the desert days. They "set bounds to the Holy One of Israel." They made an idol of God.

Felix Adler, founding the Society for Ethical Culture in 1876, felt that it continued the religious tradition, without superstition and without idolatry; as the legend above the speaker's platform reads, "The place where men meet to seek the highest is holy ground."

When the Ethical Culture movement was young a member boasted that it was the first religion based on a passion for righteousness. The eminent Rabbi Emil Hirsch answered that there was a religion founded some three thousand years ago by one Moses that was based on a passion for righteousness. Matthew Arnold fastened the ethical emphasis on Judaism in his *Literature and Dogma.* "The Righteous Eternal loveth righteousness": "Conduct is three-fourths of life and conduct is Hebraism."

But does Judaism say that God is righteous, or that God is

God? Does it aim to do right, or to do the will of God? ("Even from everlasting to everlasting, Thou art God.")

Little Samuel answered the human voice that called him in the night: "Speak, Lord, for Thy servant heareth." Isaiah responds eagerly to the divine query on whom to send with the message: "Here am I; send me."

The first petition in the brief model prayer is "Thy Kingdom come, Thy will be done." Mary answers the angelic salutation, "Behold the handmaid of the Lord; be it unto me according to thy word." Paul accedes to the heavenly vision: "Lord, what wilt thou have me to do?" Defending himself before Agrippa (Herod Agrippa II) Paul tells how immediate was his response: "Whereupon, O King Agrippa, I was not disobedient unto the heavenly vision." The divine will motivates the garden scene. The eternal high priest comes quoting Psalms: "I come to do Thy will, O God."

The third famous Gamaliel in the House of Hillel is memorialized in the *Sayings of the Fathers* on this point of doctrine: "Make His will as thy will, that He may make thy will as His Will." (Pirke Aboth 2:4.)

"A people prepared for the Lord" can have no purpose but to serve the Lord. "There was a people that would do His will! Stubborn—they would need to be stubborn!" Bishop Alma White penetrated the magic and the mystery of Israel's election.

Moses before the mount addressed himself to all the generations of Israel. Paul on Mars' Hill speaks to the Gentile world. He lacks neither daring nor grace. His theme is the Living God who has one altar—the heart of man.

As Paul waited in Athens for Silas and Timothy to join him, he looked about the city, and his spirit was stirred within him. At the beauty of the architecture? (All the buildings erected by Pericles were still standing.) At all the idolatry! If the young Lucius pointed out Lesbos to Paul as their ship ran along the Greek isles on the last journey to Jerusalem ("There's where Sappho lived! There's Mitylene"), what interest did he evoke? Only the thought of a soul that wanted salvation?

The incurious among Paul's first audience in the Athenian market place are ready to dismiss Paul and his message, but the more eager in the thirst for knowledge of the religion of others lead him courteously to the Hill of Mars. One of Paul's converts is Dionysius, a member of the council of the Areopagus.

When Paul speaks of the resurrection, some scoff, but others desire to hear more. It is not unheard of to them that God should raise the dead. Hercules brought back Alcestis from the tomb; Orpheus, Eurydice; Hermes, Persephone. Protesilaus came back to spend one hour with Laodamia. Dionysus lay dead and buried at Delphi, with the inscription on his tomb, "Here lies Dionysus dead, the son of Semele," and was reincarnated in the omophagic rite. Castor and Pollus alternated in life and death. The infant Zeus was born every year on the island of Crete, where the grave of Idaean Zeus was also marked.

> Methought I saw my late-espoused saint
> Brought to me like Alcestis from the grave,

wrote the Puritan lover of all sacred song.

Some philosophers of the Epicurean and Stoic schools, the most materialistic schools of Greece, deride Paul as a "beggarly babbler." Weymouth has "this seed-picker," "this grain-gatherer," putting Paul in the distinguished company of the "corn-bearer" Ammonius Saccas (pagan or Christian?), teacher of the most famous of the pagan neo-Platonists, Plotinus, and the most prolific of the patristic writers, Origen.

Paul sings the paean of that God whom the author of the Vedic hymn had sung one thousand years before, whom the Stoic Cleanthes had sung a quarter of a millennium back, whom Philo hymns in Paul's day. ("Some of your own poets have said . . .")

God, who has made from one all nations of men ("from one forefather," "from one blood"), now calls on all men "to change their minds." Once only to judge themselves against the appointed day of judgment before that Man whom God has predestined to the work and signalized by raising him from the dead.

Philo in the name of Moses issues the universal call to repentance and return to God.

The most holy Moses, being a lover of virtue, and of honor, and, above all things, of the human race, expects all men everywhere to show themselves admirers of piety and of justice, proposing to them, as to conquerors, great rewards if they repent, namely, a participation in the best of all constitutions, and an enjoyment of all things, whether great or small, which are to be found in it. (*On Repentance* I.1)

"Moses," continues Philo, in the discourse *On Three Virtues* —courage, humanity, repentance—"Moses delivers to us very beautiful exhortations to repentance by which he teaches us to alter our way of life."

And the first thing to repent is not to have served the one only God—the Creator instead of His creatures.

For as when the sun arises the darkness disappears and all places are filled with light, so in the same manner when God, that sun appreciable only by the intellect, arises and illuminates the soul, the whole darkness of vices and passions is dissipated, and the pure and lovely appearance of bright and radiant virtues is displayed to the world. (Philo III, *On Humanity*, 22.2)

Paul makes known the riches of glory in the "mystery" of Christ hidden for ages from all men.

The most celebrated of the Greek mysteries was Demeter's the "Earth Mother," the Corn Mother whose daughter, the golden-haired Corn Maiden, Persephone, became the bride of Death.

> A mortal ripens like corn,
> like corn he springs up again.
> (*Katha-Upanishad* I.1.6)

> That which thou sowest
> is not quickened, except it die. (I Cor. 15:36)

The mourning mother had ordered a temple to be built to her at Eleusis upon the jutting crags overlooking Salamis and the sea.

She showed them the manner of her rites, and taught them her
goodly mysteries, holy mysteries which none may violate, or
search into, or noise abroad, for the great curse from the Gods
restrains the voice. Happy is he among deathly men who hath
beheld these things; and he that is uninitiate, and hath no lot
in them, hath never equal lot in death beneath the murky gloom.
(*Homeric Hymns,* Hymn to Demeter, pp. 209–10)

When John Wesley discomfited the Anglican clergy by his
insistence on a definite experience of conversion, one divine called
it a revival of the Eleusinian mysteries. Wesley did not take it as
a compliment, nor was it intended as such.

It is a call to a better Wisdom and a better Word than the
Greeks have known—a clearer and a cleaner mystery—when Paul
presents the Savior "who of God is made unto us wisdom and
righteousness and sanctification and redemption."

Was the mystery never an essential expression of the rational
Greek soul? Homer knows of the mystery, but he exhibits no interest in the theme of salvation. Diomed challenges Glaucus on the
battlefield with the instance of Lycurgus. He will fight any but
the gods of Heaven. Brave Lycurgus drew down the punishment
of Zeus and the hate of all the gods for pursuing the "nurses of
Dionysus," the maenads, with an ox-goad through Nyssa, their
holy ground, and chasing the terrified wine-god into the sea.

Was the rational never the interpretation of life for the
greater part of the Greeks? *The Bacchanals* of Euripides (also
Bacchae: Bacchantes) expresses the division in the Greek consciousness. King Pentheus repeats the libel on the maenads, among
whom are the women of his own family, and vows to imprison
them all and slay the new god who has appeared in Thebes from
the land of Lydia:

> . . . Beauteous with golden locks and purple cheeks,
> Eyes moist with Aphrodite's melting fire.
> And day and night he is with the throng, to guile
> Young maidens to the soft inebriate rites.

The blind seer Tiresias holds abstention from the rites to be
contempt of the gods:

No wile, no paltering with the deities.
The ancestral faith, coeval with our race,
No subtle reasoning, if it soar aloft
Even to the height of wisdom, can o'erthrow.

(Euripides: *Bacchanals*)

Dionysus in disguise takes Pentheus to view the forbidden rites, where the women, divinely possessed, led by his own mother, tear him to pieces. This is only part of the punishment designed by the fates for the impiety of the House of Thebes, and delivered by the mildest of the gods to men.

Were the ugliest things in the mystery most Greek? Those darker emotions which Euripides reveals in *The Bacchanals* are glossed with loveliness in our English poets. Except for the trailing ivy, and crown of leaf and flower, we hardly recognize the mystic votaries of Swinburne in these Bacchantes with serpents playing about their heads, tearing their living victims to pieces, or snatching up the young of kid or goat to suckle instead of the infant left at home.

There are sunless chasms in the Greek soul. Wesley, perusing Xenophon's *Memorabilia,* comes on some things about Socrates that he thinks the artistic judgment of Plato would have left unsaid: "But it may be well that we see the shades too of the brightest picture in all heathen antiquity."

Plato knows that "God is perfectly simple and true."[3] Man's aim should be to be like Him. But how to effectuate the divine in life he knows not. Plato would not allow love for a slave in the house except in holy marriage. He can only suggest the building up of a tradition as firm as the natural sentiment against incest. The sanctification of life he has not truly learned—the utter devotion of soul and body to God.

Be ye holy, for I am holy. I the Lord thy God am holy.

Socrates dies rather than to disobey the will of God and give up his heavenly calling of examining men. They felt his power and were ashamed before him. But neither Socrates nor Plato,

---

[3] *The Republic,* book II, p. 82; compare *Laws* IV.2, pp. 420–21.

"the divine," had the authority to issue the unequivocal command: "Be ye therefore perfect, even as your Father which is in Heaven is perfect."

Aristotle tells the story of the winner in the Olympic contest who fled in horror from his mother's love, but took his too-dear friend with him—the future lawgiver of Thebes.

Virtue equals the order of love, affection, charity, in Augustine's *City of God* (XV.22.4). He quotes the Canticle of Canticles (2:4) literally: "His banner over me [is] love." *"Ordinavit in me charitatem,"* reads the Vulgate after the Greek Bible. "He set love [agape] in order in me." ("Though I speak with the tongues of men and of angels, and have not charity . . . and have not love [agape] . . .")

To love right things and to love them rightly, is not this to have found the salvation of God?

MAN AND NATURE: SYMBOLISM

TO THE pagan soul the Jew might easily seem an atheist, with his almost imageless worship and nature divested of everything divine. The classic pagan moved in a world of familiar enchantments. Nymphs dwelt in tree and field and stream, and gods roamed the world. If the Jew felt a conscious life interfused through visible nature he referred it all to the Living God, whose glory the heavens declare, in whose praise the floods lift up their voice, and whose being is imaged in the works of His hands.

Homer's famous anthropomorphism may be largely a poet's pantheism—not man in nature but God in nature. The corn, the oil, the wine, are holy beings: a god is in the wine cup, nor would any drink before first pouring to a god the unmixed wine.

All nature is divinely animated. If Achilles' horses can respond to his address and prophesy his death on the Plains of Troy, it is not in assumption of a human attribute, but because they are divine:

> The gods themselves,
> Humbling their deities to love, have taken
> The shapes of beasts upon them; Jupiter
> Became a bull, and bellowed; the green Neptune
> A ram, and bleated; and the fire-robed god,
> Golden Apollo, a poor humble swain.
>
> (*The Winter's Tale*, IV.4)

To ancient eyes the gods do not demean themselves to take on the guise of any beast. Proteus assumed every animal shape in attempting to escape Menelaus' grasp. In reminiscence of an earlier day, Juno is still the ox-eyed queen, and Jupiter bellowed as a bull in the primitive suit of Europa the cow. The noble centaurs who taught the divine heroes were both man and horse. Paris goes out in his glorious armor like a proud horse breaking away from the stalls to seek pleasant companionship in the fields; none the less is he "god-like." If the Egyptian deities were not animals to the last, most of them retained an animal feature.

"Doth God take care for oxen?" asks Paul, but Paul is modern.

Baruch inserts in a praise of wisdom, and the light, and the dutiful stars an affectionate notice of the lower creation. "He that prepared the earth for evermore hath filled it with four-footed beasts." And how respectfully the prophet answers the complaint of the ass!

Is not God a tender shepherd? Did He not pity the cattle as well as the innocent babies in the city of Nineveh? Is not His altar a refuge for the birds? Does not the beast of burden enjoy the Sabbath rest and share in the ultimate redemption of all creation to the first divine order? Does not the promise to Noah after the Flood extend to every living thing that lives upon the earth? Francis interpreted Scripture literally when he preached to the birds and the fish and the beasts and converted the wolf of Gubbio.

The very landscape reflects the difference between pantheistic Greece, in effect polytheistic, and monotheistic Judea.. The shrines and altars, the heaps of stones at the crossroads, increased by each traveler as a votive offering to Hermes, friend of the wayfarer—all were evidences that the philosophers had failed, because they were themselves bound, where the priests and the prophets had triumphed.

The image that is not an object of worship is not idolatrous. Moses set up the brazen serpent on a pole as an antidote to the serpent's sting, although he had so strictly forbidden anyone to "make unto himself" any image of any living thing.

The wing tips of the cherubim touched over the Mercy Seat in the Holiest Place. The horns of the altar at least suggested the victim of sacrifice. Solomon had two lions guarding his ivory and gold throne, and lions flanking each of the six steps.

The molten sea of brass about the brazen altar rested on twelve oxen and the brim of the basin was ornamented with two rows of three hundred oxen. But not for these things was Solomon an idolater.

Homer finds in the life of the tree a sympathetic parallel to the life of man; and if the generations of man pass like the leaves, he is the sadder wanting the faith that like the leaves they will come again.

> Like the race of leaves
> Is that of humankind. Upon the ground
> The winds strew one year's leaves; the sprouting grove
> Puts forth another brood, that shoot and grow
> In the spring season. So it is with man:
> One generation grows while one decays.

As Homer feels no partisanship for the heroes in combat, hating Mars but loving the fight, so he does not take man's side against nature, nor use nature as a mere typology for man.

Two primitive idolatries are enshrined in Coleridge's hymn to Mont Blanc and in Bryant's "Forest Hymn." The voices of both Law and Prophecy thunder against the heart lifted up in worship of the creature instead of the Creator. Still, "the groves were God's first temples," and before man knew a word for God he looked for comfort to the hills. The hardest idolatries for the prophets to uproot were the worship of the mountains and the trees. The Babylonian Ishtar, goddess of fertility and of love, is associated in the prophets with the symbol of the grove, the *ashera*. ("Upon every high hill, and under every green tree, thou wanderest, playing the harlot.")

The earliest parable in the Bible is Jotham's fable of the trees of the forest choosing a king. Solomon spoke of trees, from the cedar in Lebanon to the hyssop springing in the wall. The blessed life is like a tree by the watercourse thriving in its native soil. Sirach calls the high priest Simon as he stands to minister before the altar a flourishing cedar of Lebanon, and his attendant priests graceful saplings by the brook. Israel is that vine transplanted out of Egypt which has taken deep root and spread out branches mighty as the cedar. This Jewish race so often uprooted is at home in every soil. The cedar is most often used to typify the Jewish spiritual ideal: firm-rooted in the earth, with branches that spread as wide as the tree reaches upward, an incorruptible wood, a tree made to live forever.

> Ye spread and span like the catholic man who hath mightily won
> God out of knowledge and good out of infinite pain
> And sight out of blindness and purity out of a stain.
>
> (Lanier, *The Marshes of Glynn*)

Which was the greater marvel of creation? The ranges of Lebanon and Anti-Lebanon on the northern boundary of Israel, or the ageless trees that covered their sides—the trees that God had planted? The Indians gave the name deodar, or god-tree, to the cedar that grew in the holy places in the Himalayas. The Japanese built their temple among the aspiring cryptomerias at Nikko, but the cedars were a temple before anything was built there. The Druids celebrated their mysteries under

> The mythic oaks . . .
> Self-poised upon their prodigy of shade.
>
> (E. B. Browning, *Aurora Leigh*)

Jewish tradition set the first lovers in the "green mansions" of the happy forest, God's own husbandry in which He took delight. Prophetic hyperbole calls Assyria the fairest tree in the Garden of God. The restored Temple of Zion will be glorious with the beauty of Lebanon, with cypress, plane tree, larch—glorious with trees.

And when the thunder roll of Prophecy has died the rabbi asks, "What must we say when we see the first leaves on the tree in the spring?" We must say, "Blessed be God who hath created such a being."

It must have been man's persistent sympathy with nature that led at last to the discovery of the being of a God—of the Creator in the creature. In the orderly process of the heavens he read his part in a high enterprise, and in the near, familiar things of nature he felt a divine solicitude.

Did the trees teach man to hope and pray, the hills to abide
in faith? Did the stars teach him to sing "Gloria"?

The idol renounced is resumed as the symbol. God's righteousness is "like" the mountains of God. The one holy place is "the
Mountain of the Lord's House," and the tree becomes the redeeming Cross. What more apt symbol for the life of man than the
tree?

"As the days of a tree are the days of my people"—the symbol
of prosperity—but "cursed is everyone that hangeth on a tree"—
the symbol of defeat and ultimate agony. Christ took on himself
the curse of the Law and turned the sign of infamy into the sign
of salvation. "Death is swallowed up in victory" (I Cor. 15:54).

The cross was known from India to Scandinavia. It is in the
Buddhist list of the miseries of life. As far as the northern
headland of Europe the swastika, the Aryan cross, was the symbol
of the sun-god. The Egyptian ankh, borne by the god, was the
symbol of enduring life, of generation. The Jew made the cross
the symbol of *regeneration* for those *reborn* of incorruptible seed
by the Word of God.

Only the Latin had a distinct word for cross, our word *crux*.
The cross remained the tree, or the stake, sometimes a standing
tree. The word is wanting, but the institution is universal. Too
many had died so. When Alexander took Tyre he put eight or
ten thousand to the sword and two thousand crosses along the
shore served for an object lesson: Open your gates to Alexander.
And Alexander was the noblest of all the world conquerors!

After the third Servile War (71 B.C.), led by Spartacus, who
died in battle, the Romans lined the Appian Way with crosses.
(Let the slaves know that Romans are born to rule!) And
during the siege of Jerusalem (A.D. 70) five hundred fugitives
were daily impaled along what was once the wall of the city.
Titus pitied them but he could neither guard nor release so many.

Nor did the Jews learn the custom of the Romans. The
reprehensible Alexander Jannaeus (104/3–78/6 B.C.), returned
to power through the Jews' loyalty to the Maccabean house,

paid off the Pharisees who had withstood its secularization. This man, who ministered as high priest before the altar, doomed eight hundred of his former opponents to crosses to die of suffocation and thirst, and slew their families before their eyes. Quintilius Varus, president of the province of Syria, punished "some of the most guilty" in a revolt in Judea and crucified two thousand men. Titus could put on a show at Caesarea in honor of his brother's birthday in which twenty-five hundred captives were to die. For his father's birthday he achieved a greater spectacle at Berytus (Beirut), a Roman colony in Phoenicia.

Herod Agrippa I, a prospective messiah, showed his favor to the townspeople of Berytus and built an amphitheater in which he staged a gladiatorial combat with seven hundred men on a side in the mimic war. He was able to find fourteen hundred men who ought to die.

Above that welter of blood and tears stands out the Cross of Christ. Christ bearing the cross—the too heavy burden: there is a symbol that everyone understands. And man not only bears his cross, but he yields his life on it at the last. The Jew is not the only one who wakes out of a cloud of myrrh to find himself fixed on a cross. The sorrows of life are for all men. "So must the son of man be lifted up."

The old bishop in Oscar Wilde's story "The Young Prince" tells the prince who has resolved to wear nothing at his coronation that has caused human suffering: "The burden of this world is too great for one man to bear, and the world's sorrow too heavy for one heart to suffer." But the consolation of the Cross is that a human heart did once bear sympathetically the sorrows of all men forever, did once recapitulate the whole history of human suffering.

> Yea, once Immanuel's orphaned cry
>   his universe hath shaken—
> It went up single, echoless, "My
>   God, I am forsaken!"
>
> It went up from the Holy's lips
>   amid his lost creation,

That, of the lost, no son should use
those words of desolation,
That earth's worst phrenzies, marring
hope, should mar not hope's fruition.
(E. B. Browning, *Cowper's Grave*)

Cut into the outer wall of the Black Pagoda (black because deserted), the only part left of the ruined thirteenth-century temple to the old Vedic sun-god Surya, there is a group of figures known as "the Apsaras humbling an ascetic." The half-divine nymphs, spirits of clouds and waters, born of the churning of ocean, are teaching the ascetic that he is no different from other men. The instruction is most explicit. Here is the interwoven phallic and serpent symbol that appears in the Edenic tale, where the serpent typifies both woman and man and the union of two.

Universally the Sun is a male deity, and the Moon female. The fire on the altar and the sticks that start the fire are male and female. The Indian Shakespeare, Kalidasa, describes in the *Shakuntala* how the heroine, the mother of Bharata, epic hero of the *Mahabharata,* quitting her garden for the home of her divine husband, leaves the vine she had tended with sisterly devotion in the care of a neighbor tree, because sex prevades all things and all things know the attraction of love.

The most obvious symbol of the fertility of all nature is the phallus. The Vedic symbol becomes in the Hindu Shiva worship (Dionysus) an idol. Shiva's consort, identified with the "Good Mother," Ambika, and known by many names—among them Devi, the Goddess; Mahadevi, the Great Goddess, Parvati, the Daughter of the Mountains—is worshipped in the complementary representation to the lingam, the yoni—a prism.

A phallic procession opened the religious festival of the Dionysia at Athens, in which each Athenian colony participated, bearing the symbol. The celebration of the Dionysia was the beginning of the Greek drama. The Greek myth recounts the very fleshly origin of Aphrodite, "Queen of Smiles," "Lady of Laughter."

The *Avesta* employs the one symbol for fertility in man and nature. "Unhappy is the land that has long lain unsown with the seed of the sower and wants a good husbandman, like a well-shapen maiden who has long gone childless and wants a good husband" (*Vendidad* III.III.24).

The earth will yield her good fruits to the tiller as to her lover. To plant the earth is to suckle the religion of Mazda.

> When you shall be come into the land, and shall have planted in it fruit trees, you shall take away the first fruits of them: the fruit that comes forth shall be unclean to you, neither shall you eat of them.

The newly planted trees are uncircumcised and unclean until the *praeputia,* the foreskins, have been removed. After the fruits are offered to God, they are sanctified, as in circumcision, and available for the use of man.

The Chinese mystic, attempting to characterize "the quiet but mighty influence of the impersonal Tao," even calls it "the Mother of all things." (*Tao Teh King* I.1.1.)

> Who is your lady of love . . . ?
>
> Our lady of love by you is unbeholden,
> For hands she hath none, nor eyes, nor lips nor golden
> Treasure of hair, nor face nor form;
> But we
> That love, we know her more fair than anything.
>
> (Swinburne, *The Pilgrims*)

*   *   *

The juice of the heavenly plant that confers immortality on gods and men is known to the Indian as soma, to the Iranian as haoma, and to the Greek as ambrosia. (The Sanskrit amrita is the Greek amarant, "undying.") Milton pictures the angels in Heaven:

> Their crowns inwove with amarant and gold;
> Immortal amarant, a flower which once
> In Paradise, fast by the tree of life,
> Began to bloom; but soon for man's offense
> To Heaven removed where first it grew.

Zoroaster inquires of Ahura Mazda with what sacrifice to

worship or to make people worship God's creation. Mazda directs him to the high-growing trees. Before a beautiful and mighty tree the priest is to say,

> Hail to thee!
> O good, holy tree, made by Mazda!

and repeat the "Praise of Holiness":

> Holiness is the best of all good; it is also happiness. Happy the man who is holy with perfect holiness!
> Well is it for it, well is it for that holiness which is perfection of holiness. (*Vendidad* XIX.3,4)

Then the priest cuts the twig of baresma from the tree. When he prays and when he offers the oblation, the golden haoma, before the sacred fire, the priest holds the consecrated bundle of baresma in his hand, most aptly when he prays for increase to Mithra (Apollo), the Light. The worshipper keeps his eye on the baresma. It is to him "a tree of life." The "bunch of hyssop" serves like the bundle of baresma for purification in some of the Mosaic ritual (II Macc. 14:3-4).

The ex-high-priest Alcimus presented to Demetrius I (162 B.C.), successor of Antiochus V (Eupator), gifts in the hope of regaining the high priesthood, which he had lost to the Maccabees—a crown of gold, a palm, and some of the boughs "which were used solemnly in the Temple." The rededication of the Temple after its desecration by Antiochus IV is celebrated (II Macc. 10:5-8) with branches, fair boughs and palms as ordained in Leviticus for the congregation to bring to the Feast of Tabernacles, and interpreted by the rabbis to mean the ceremonial lulab of thick myrtle and willow bound up with the folded palm.

Conspicuous above the door of Herod's Temple was a golden vine hanging down in large branches. A branch with a cluster of grapes represented the golden bough in the Greek vintage festival, the Oschophoria.

The flourishing bough with its formal representation, the Maypole, is familiar in European custom. The Puritans' objection to the Maypole was that they saw in it the *ashera* of the Canaanites.

The sacred bough confers immunity. Agamemnon's threat to Chryses, Apollo's priest, who comes bearing the suppliant's bough —the golden staff and fillets of the god—and offering large ransom for his daughter, brings down on the Greek host a pestilence that can be stayed only by the sending of a hecatomb and the return of Chryseis without ransom.

The blind seer Tiresias meets Odysseus on his expedition to the world below bearing the golden wand.

Aeneas, repeating Odysseus' adventure in the realms where none living may pass, has for safe-conduct the golden branch the Sibyl bears concealed, the hallowed present to the dread queen, torn from the holm-oak in the dark forest on the verge of hell.

The sacred bough confers fertility. Calpurnia stands where the runner wearing the wreath, bearing the bough, may touch her in his course. Before the degradation of the custom, the Spartan boys in the temple of Artemis had but to endure one stroke of the sacred bough. The wreath was worn by the contestants in the Greek games to prosper them. The winner at Olympia was crowned with wild olive—the felicitous, the fecund olive, Virgil calls it. The wild olive of the Gentiles is fructified by grafting on the good olive tree of Judaism in Paul's allegory. The contestants in the games practice temperance for a corruptible crown, says Peter, but the followers of Christ for the golden crown of incorruption, of purity—"a crown of glory that fadeth not away" (I Pet. 5:4).

Aaron's bare staff budded—a golden bough. The dry stock of Israel shall blossom and bud and fill the face of the world with fruitage—the golden bough among the nations. A rod out of the stem of Jesse, a branch out of his roots, is that Man Israel—My servant—THE BRANCH.

The Old English keeps the meaning and the term of a "shoot" in *rood*. The Holy Rood in the "Elene" of the *Saints' Legends* is—

> ... The fairest of trees,
> Storied and sung by sons of men,
> O'er the ways of the world.[1]

---

[1] J. D. Spaeth, *Old English Poetry*.

"Rood triumphant and incorruptible" is the "cross of life," "the victory-tree."

The Cross is a tree stripped of its leaves to which the eye of faith looks for the miracle of renascence.

THE GOSPEL OF THE POOR

A SLAVE IN Aristotle's analysis is "by nature not his own but another's man." Demosthenes, who protests much in the name of the gods, insults his opponent Aeschines: in his youth he helped his mother in the mysteries, and in his boyhood he made himself serviceable to his father "just like a slave, not like the child of a citizen."

The writer of the Sirach, misled by the Greeks, agrees that "the wisdom of a learned man cometh by opportunity of leisure."

The plowman, the smith, the potter, the artisan—the carpenter, for instance—have their only interest in serving the material wants of mankind. But a Carpenter did apply himself to the Jewish learning and wrought so well that not only his name but his every word is "for a blessing." And every plowman may read as Tyndale averred that he might, for in the scholarly service of bringing the Bible to the people many a man besides Tyndale has given his life.

The humble Carpenter—Paul, whose hands ministered to his own and others' necessities—even the Jewish God, who looked at the work of His hands and called it good—would not be honored citizens of Aristotle's Best State. The sacred mysteries were not open independently to artisan and laborer in the democratic city of Athens, that had many slaves to one citizen.

Aristotle agrees that "the Gods should receive honor from the citizens only." Mechanics, husbandmen, just as slaves or Perioeci belonging to the land, are incapable of virtuous action. Only the ruling class, the property holders, are fit to share in the state. They alone realize that happy *function* that is the perfect exercise of virtue. "The best life both for individuals and states is the life of virtue": but it is not attainable to the poor.

When Jesus, on the prophetic assumption that very slaves might know themselves as sons and daughters of the Living God, that strangers might aspire to a preferred place, and outcasts be welcomed in the House of the Lord—when Jesus issued his universal invitation to the Christian mystery, how it must have sounded in the ears of the world like an angel's song, like flute tones from afar! (Matt. 11:28–30).

"Come unto me, all ye that labour and are heavy-laden."

CREED AND DOGMA

THE conflict in the Catholic Church that was provisionally settled by the Council of Nicaea (325) with the formulation of the Apostles' Creed, named after Athanasius, repudiating Arius as a heretic, could not have arisen among the first Christians. They thought of Christ's unity with the Father, not his consubstantiality. Immaterial substance was not in their day a theme of debate in Palestine.

It is the difficult act of faith that requires a credo. The axiomatic statement hardly needs to be erected into a dogma. The Hebrew "God is God" like the Eleatic "One is One" is not susceptible of proof, and behind these no man can go.[1]

The Sirach repeats the Psalmist's warning against trying things that are too hard. The early rabbis echoed Ben Sira and discouraged any inquiry into the works of creation or the "mystery" expressed in the "chariot" of Ezekiel.

The translator of the *Kazari,* Hartwig Hirschfeld, is vehement in denial of dogma to Judaism, even though he grants an incipient creed to Philo in the five lessons of Moses: "God has real existence. God is one. The world is created. The world is one. God's providence embraces the world." Even though there is implicit dogma in the Mishnah when it denies a part in future happiness to the one who asserts that the resurrection of the dead is not in the Torah, that the Torah is not of divine origin—and to the heretic—still Hirschfeld maintains that "articles of creed in any shape are not of Jewish growth." The Thirteen Articles "encroached upon the Jewish prayer book." The "I believe" was

---

1 Aristotle, *Metaphysics* 1.5; Plato IV: *Sophist,* p. 345; *Parmenides,* p. 315.

the addition of the first Hebrew translator, and the "with perfect faith," a liturgical ornament.

The commentary from the Mishnah, based on Isaiah 60:21, "All Israelites have a portion in the world to come," rendered also, "The righteous of all nations have a share in the world to come," leads Maimonides to the Thirteen Articles of the Jewish faith—the metrical *Yigdal* of the prayer book:

> *Yigdal Elohim hai ve yishtabach*:
> Extolled be the Living God and praised.

Doctor Schechter finds dogma in Judaism and cites rabbinic authorities: among them Judah Halevi, Maimonides, Nachmanides, all in the circle of Arabic thought who take the announcement "I am the Lord thy God" as a command to believe in His existence.

It was largely in answer to Moslem theologians that Judah Halevi (Abul Hassan), the Castilian poet, wrote about 1140 his defense of historic rabbinic Judaism, the *Kitab al Khazari*, "The Book of the Kazars," a "book of argument and demonstration in aid of the despised faith," making use of a little-known historic event—the conversion four hundred years before of the king of the Khazars, a powerful Turanian tribe of southern Russia.

The Moslems have three sacred books—the Old Testament, the New Testament, and the Koran. If the Koran borrows its light from the Bible as the moon from the sun, the moon also ennobles what it illumes.

The Koran establishes Ismael as co-heir of Abraham, who thanks God for both his boys: "Praise be unto God who hath given me, in my old age, Ismael and Isaac: for my Lord is the hearer of supplication." (K. XIV.38; tr. Sale.)

Jacob at the point of death asks his sons, "Whom will ye worship after me?" and they answer, "We will worship thy God, and the God of thy fathers Abraham, and Ismael, and Isaac, one God, and to him will we be resigned." (K. II.134.)

"Abraham (the father of all the faithful) was neither a Jew nor a Christian: but he was of the true religion, one resigned unto God and was not of the number of the idolators." (K. III.66.) The favored definition of Islam is "resignation or submission to the service and commands of God." A Moslem is one resigned.

The vine transplanted out of Egypt bore branches mighty as the cedar. Like the true vine of the parable, yet unbroken, it gives its strength to the priestly tradition of Catholicism, which continues the daily sacrifice, the daily renewal of the covenant with God; to the prophetic tradition in the Protestant churches, which writes the new convenant in each man's heart; to the rigid monotheism of Islam, which never ceases to iterate how that God is most great, and how that there is no God but God.

A century back, George Sale introduced his English translation of the Koran with misgivings that he might be thought to be presenting a rival to the Christian Scriptures, manifest forgery though it be. Yet Sale deplores his own inability to render into English the many passages, sublime and magnificent, especially those that describe the majesty and attributes of God.

The Bible is not an oasis in the arid desert of the human spirit, but an enchanted isle in the infinite ocean of fine thoughts and generous feelings.

"Thy way of thinking is indeed pleasing to the Creator, but not thy way of acting," said the angel in the dream; and now the king of the Kazars summons first a philosopher (an Arab Aristotelian), then a Christian Scholastic and a faithful Moslem, satisfied that the Jews are too insignificant to be worth consulting.

The philosopher answers that the Prime Cause manifests no will and therefore no purpose toward man. In regard to the theory and practice of faith, the Scholastic answers that the Church is the true Israel, the Twelve Apostles are the Twelve Tribes, and that Christ did not abrogate the Law. The Moslem says that Mohammed superseded all previous laws and that the Koran is a miracle because not imitable in any verse. But there must be a sign from Heaven to prove that God speaks to man. "Is not our Book full of the stories of Moses and the children of Israel?" Now the king feels compelled to consult the Jews, although "aware of their reduced condition and narrow-minded views, as their misery left them nothing commendable."

The Scholastic had begun: "I believe that all things are created, whilst the Creator is eternal." The Moslem: "We acknowledge the unity and eternity of God." The rabbi goes straight to the point of his Jewishness: "I believe in the God of Abraham, Isaac and Israel, who led the children of Israel out of Egypt with signs and miracles"—who exhibited His concern in all their subsequent history. "Our belief is comprised in the Torah —a very large domain."

The king makes most astute inquiries which the rabbi answers triumphantly for Judaism. "This religion—it was a long, gradual growth. . . . Some individual first, perhaps, then a few. . . . Finally a king lent his aid." No. "A religion of divine origin arises suddenly. It is bidden to arise, and it is there like the creation of the world." ("God only says to a thing be, and it is" [K. III.47].) As for Aristotle, "he exerted his mind because he had no tradition from any reliable source." With a Semitic inheritance he would have argued for the creation, however difficult to prove, instead of the eternity of matter, which is still more difficult.

"One hearing of how God spoke with the assembled multitude and wrote tables for you might take it that you personify God." "Heaven forbid."

"The first of the Ten Commandments enjoins the belief in Divine Providence. The second command contains the prohibition of the worship of other gods, or the association of any being with Him, the prohibition to represent Him in statues, forms and images, or any personification of Him." Many of His creations are above that—"the human soul, which represents man's true essence." As Halevi has drawn on the Arabs he can draw on the Greeks. Not Moses' tongue, heart, or brain taught, but Moses himself—"intellectual, discriminating, incorporeal soul, not limited by place, neither too large, nor too small, for any space in order to contain the images of all creatures. If we ascribe spiritual elements to it, how much more must we do so to the Creator of all?"

The philosopher only seeks a description of God. In the conclusion the rabbi draws a final contrast between the faithful of the Jews and philosophers: "We dwell on His works but refrain from describing His nature. For if we were able to grasp it, this were a defect in Him."

Philosophy concerns itself with Godhead, religion with God.

A Christian scholar asks the ardent Maimonist, the rabbi Abraham ben Shem-Tob Bibago, at the table of John II of Aragón, (father of Ferdinand II of Aragón, Ferdinand V of Castile), "Are you the Jewish philosopher?"

"I am a Jew who believes in the Law given to us by our teacher Moses, though I have studied philosophy."[2] Never can worldly learning match with the divine Torah.

> Let her know her place;
> She is the second, not the first.

The earlier Humanism was the rebirth of classic Latin literature. Dante chose his fellow countryman Virgil to conduct his journey through Hell and Purgatory. Only beyond the Earthly Paradise where no pagan might enter must he choose another guide, the divine Beatrice.

The later Humanism came inevitably to the prime sources in Greek and Hebrew. Reuchlin, great-uncle of Luther's coadjutor Melanchthon and defender of the rabbinic learning, was the author of the first Hebrew grammar composed by a non-Jew. Another true Humanist was the Dutch Erasmus (Desiderius Erasmus Roterodamus, *ca.* 1466-1536), who sought the victories of peace knowing the dangers of conflict. While Luther was posting his Theses, and being drawn on by wily disputants, excommunicated, banned by the Empire, summoned to defend himself before a church council, Erasmus was diligently working on the text of his parallel Greek and Latin New Testament. While Luther thundered and hammered at indulgences, Erasmus concerned himself to discover in a Greek manuscript one attestation to the three heavenly witnesses of I John 5:7.

---

[2] Solomon Schechter, *Studies in Judaism,* I, 172–73.

Erasmus consistently refused to enter the lists against the reformers or even to act as mediator. His interest was literature. Only at last (1524) did he come out against Luther in *De Libero Arbitrio* ("On Free Will") in the cause dearest to his heart, "to vindicate the dignity and liberty of the human spirit."

Where in the Old Testament does one ask another, "Dost thou believe?" The trumpet is blown in Zion and the announcement made: Hear, O Israel, thus saith the Lord your God . . .

"If thou canst believe," Jesus says to the father of the afflicted boy, and the father answers, "Lord, I believe; help thou mine unbelief."

"Believest thou this?" Jesus asks Martha when he makes his dogmatic statement of the fundamental doctrine of the Christian faith.

A Pharisaic Jew knows that the dead will live again in the resurrection on the last day. But Jesus had made the Christian not the Jewish profession:

"I am the resurrection and the life: he that believeth in me, though he were dead, yet shall he live: and whosoever liveth and believeth in me shall never die. Believest thou this?". . .

"Yea, Lord, I believe." (John 11:25–27)

All the intense personality of Jewish thinking gathered up and centered in this new confession of faith!

("Do you accept Jesus Christ as *your own personal Savior?*")

RHETORIC AND RELIGION

AURELIUS AUGUSTINUS was born November 13, 354, at Tagaste, Numidia, and died August 28, 430, Bishop of Hippo, while the Vandals were breaking into the city.

Augustine tells in the *Confessions* the story of the former teacher of rhetoric, Victorinus, who had merited a statue in the Roman Forum, now forbidden to teach by Julian's edict against Christian professors in the liberal arts and sciences. Augustine had been reading Victorinus' Latin translation of some works of the neo-Platonists, and when in Milan had expressed his misgivings about them to Simplicianus, successor to Bishop Ambrose of Milan in 397. Simplicianus reassured him: "The Platonists many ways led to the belief in God and His Word."

This same Victorinus, while still a pagan professor at Rome, "used to read the Holy Scripture, most studiously sought and searched into all the Christian writings," and would often say to Simplicianus, "Understand that I am already a Christian," and Simplicianus as often replied, "I will not believe it, nor will I rank you among Christians, unless I see you in the Church of Christ." Victorinus continued the banter, "Do walls then make Christians?" With sudden resolution (it is the same story that Newman tells in the *Apologia*), "Go we to the Church; I wish to be made a Christian." Victorinus becomes a catechumen and then gives in his name as desiring baptism, "Rome wondering, the Church rejoicing," and makes public profession of his faith.

Victorinus' story inspired Augustine to imitation. Augustine was also a teacher of rhetoric—in his native Tagaste, in Carthage, in Rome, and now in Milan. It was Cicero's *Hortensius,* now lost, that first excited his interest in philosophy. From the age of nineteen to twenty-eight Augustine was a Manichaean. Manichaeism was not properly a Christian heresy, but a rival Gnostic system that divided the Mediterranean world of the fourth century with neo-Platonism and Christianity.

At twenty-nine in Milan, Augustine "doubting of everything, and wavering between all" was a catechumen in the Catholic church to which his parents belonged. His mother, Monica, was an ardent Christian, his father a belated convert. Augustine tells of his experience of conversion when at the age of thirty-one, deeply distracted by the contradictions in his own nature, he heard a youthful voice chanting: "Take up and read; take up and read." He went back to where he had left the volume of the Apostle whose works he loved most of all the venerable writings of the Holy Spirit, and taking the omens from the book he read a command to leave off his vices and "put on the Lord Jesus Christ."

In the vintage season of the year 386—a golden summer that bore golden fruit—Augustine gave up "the selling of words" and wrote from his retirement in the country to Ambrose to ask what Scriptures were best to read in preparation for receiving the grace of baptism. (They took their profession of religion seriously in those days.) At Easter time in 387, Augustine, now in his thirty-third year, with a varied experience in religion, was baptized by Ambrose with his friend Alypius and his son Adeodatus, not quite fifteen, but a lad so gifted and graced that Augustine confesses he had no part in him but the sin, for "he was born after the flesh."

It was still a daring thing to be a Christian. Augustine reproves Porphyry, editor of the most famous of the pagan neo-Platonists, Plotinus, for cowardice in not being able to cover the short distance that lay between them. If the Platonists and others would only forbear to "wander off into questions they would know their God as our God."

As Augustine expounds Porphyry's three principles or hypostases that purify the soul, we see how near was the belief of pagan to Christian Platonist. "Of these he [Porphyry] called one God the Father, another God the Son, whom he termed the Mind of the Father, and between these two he placed God the Holy Ghost." Porphyry believes that the Mind, the Intellect of

God, purifies from ignorance and vices, not rites of initiation; only Porphyry cannot admit Christ to be that Mind.

Augustine's spiritual adviser, Ambrose, rebuked Theodosius after the massacre at Thessalonica (390) as Nathan the prophet had rebuked David, and, in a letter written in his own hand for Theodosius alone to read, called for a like repentance.[1] The traditional account from Theodoret, bishop of Cyrus (Cyrrhus) on the upper Euphrates, the continuator of the *Ecclesiastical History* of Eusebius, envisages Ambrose meeting Theodosius before the porch of the basilica and forbidding him, emperor of all the East (destined master of both East and West), to enter there.[2]

Ambrose explains in his letter why he could not be present, or offer the sacrifice. He would be blamed for condoning the deed, which all the bishops deplored. The episode marks the first in a new long series of dramatic encounters between the Empire of Caesar and the Kingdom of God.

Hebraism, with its monolatry, its worship of one, allows no compounding with the world. Josephus, closing his plea against Apion's libel, says in effect: "If you Gentiles will give up your vain pride in pedigree and in riches, your philosophy and your exercise of subtleties in words, which can only lead to error, and hear the inspired Prophets, the interpreters both of God and of His Word, and will believe in God, you too will attain to the smooth uplands of the heavenly kingdom; you too will experience the things of God." (Apion II.7.)

Significant for the history of literature is Jerome (*ca.* 340-420), standing at the parting of the ways to divine with the arrows—rhetoric or religion? When he renounced pagan learning and retired into the Syrian desert in preparation for the serious business of religion, he "had read the Grecian libraries," as he said Josephus seemed to have done, and now he was to make himself master of the Hebrew literature. All previous translations of the Bible converge in Jerome's Vulgate, and all subsequent European translations diverge from him.

---

[1] Ambrose's letter is in *Nicene and Post-Nicene Fathers,* 2d Series, X, 450 (Epistle 51).

[2] Theodoret in *ibid.,* 2d Series, III, book V, chapter 17, p. 143.

CHRIST AND CAESAR

IBSEN asks in *Emperor* (Caesar) *and Galilean* whether the two empires, Caesar's and the Jew's who will not die, can ever be reconciled; whether there is room on the earth for both Caesar and Jesus Christ—the eternal rebel against all that is called Caesar or Augustus. In the person of the apostate emperor Julian (361–63), Ibsen tries to reclaim the lost Greek liberty, to escape the bondage of Christ and to constitute a third empire of "World Will," fusing both.

It may have been out of a sad heart that the world turned from the sunlight of paganism to the spiritual light of the new religion. Everyone loves the sun. Everyone wants to live in the sun. No one desires the cross.

"Why was the heathen sin so beautiful?" Julian asks the Christian, who answers, "Beautiful things have been said and sung of this heathen sin; but it was not beautiful."

"Was not Alcibiades beautiful when, flushed with wine, he stormed at night like a young god through the streets of Athens? Was he not beautiful in his very audacity when he insulted Hermes and battered at the citizens' doors . . . ?"

Not so beautiful when he led 40,000 men out to die in the escapade against Syracuse (415–413 B.C.). Less beautiful when, summoned to reappear in Athens and answer to a charge of impiety for mutilating the Hermae, and profaning and divulging the Eleusinian mysteries, he betrayed the expedition to the Spartans and "fleet and army perished from the face of the earth." (Thucydides book 8, 75–87.)

If Alcibiades ever felt guilty of insolence, the sin most heinous to the Greek soul, before the hand of the Persian assassin terminated his checkered career, he could have recourse to the Greek expedient of beating his breast and blaming the gods.

It has been said that if all books were lost but Shakespeare's, a future age could not know that mankind had had a religion; but the Jewish-Christian tradition could be more easily recovered from his works than Greek religion from the whole range of the epic literature, though Homer with Hesiod be the creator of the Greek gods.

Ibsen's World Will is in sad eclipse, while Shakespeare's day does not decline. The catholic Shakespeare is orthodox in every religion. In that matchless polemic for the Jew and against the Gentile world the "unlessoned girl, unschooled, unpracticed," delivers the discourse on true religion—a page of Scripture—and the moneylending Jew pleads for our common humanity in words as authoritative as Truth itself.

Mankind would need no more religion than "sweetest Shakespeare's" for its "reasonable service" of righteousness.

TRANSLATIONS OF THE BIBLE

SEVERELY limited as Jewish learning may be, we might mark out the stages of Western culture by the translations and progress of the Bible from the Septuagint, begun (*ca.* 250 B.C.) under the patronage of Ptolemy Philadelphus as Josephus tells the story (Josephus, *Ant.* XII.II.4). The translation of the Hebrew Bible into Arabic by the Egyptian-born Saadiah (882-942), who became the head of the Academy of Sura in Babylonia, distinguishes the interval between the ancient and the modern world when the Arabs led the way in learning.

The old Gothic Bible of the Arian missionary bishop Ulfilas (Wulfila; *ca.* 350) antedates Jerome's Vulgate (*ca.* 400). Patrick first at Tara (433) dimmed with the light of the Gospel the pagan Druid altar fires, and the Saint Columba (*ca.* 565) lit in the tiny isle Iona a light of holy learning to hearten all the North. Charlemagne, who so humbly and eagerly applied himself to the rudiments of learning under Alcuin in the Palace School (782 ff.), appoints him, now abbot of St. Martin's at Tours, to emend the current Vulgate. Four Tours Bibles are credited to the editorial labor of Alcuin and his helpers about the year 800. Alfred the Great, endeavoring to elevate his people, sets himself the task of translating the Psalms into West Saxon (*ca.* 890).

The demand of the English people for a vernacular Bible such as other European nations possess gives rise to a series of versions and revisions based on the martyred Tyndale's unfinished translation from the Hebrew and the Greek (1525-34).

The more circumspect Coverdale, who was associated with Tyndale in Hamburg in 1529, brought out a complete English

Bible, including the Old Testament Apocrypha, in 1535, while Tyndale still labored in the misery of the dungeon of Vilvorde, Belgium, pending certain doom. Tyndale's many friends and the intercession of Thomas Cromwell could not prevail against the enmity of Henry VIII and Cardinal Wolsey.

The Puritan, the Geneva, Bible, dedicated to Queen Elizabeth (1560), the work of expatriates from Mary Tudor's England, was everybody's book—Shakespeare's and the book the Pilgrims brought to the new land.

Wycliff's costly manuscript Bible had been, like all the primary European vernacular Bibles, a translation of Jerome's Vulgate (N.T. 1382; O.T. 1384; John Purvey's ed. 1388).

The latest Jewish translators express their approbation of the vernacular Bibles as "a tribute to the beauty of Japheth dwelling in the spiritual tents of Israel," while Japheth on his part returns thanks in the dedication of the classic English Bible for—

That inestimable treasure which excelleth all the riches of the earth; because the fruit thereof extendeth itself not only to the time spent in this transitory world, but directeth and disposeth men unto that eternal happiness which is above in heaven.

This is the stuff of eternity.

THE MIDDLE YEARS

It is the peculiar glory of the divine Plato that all religions are translatable into his terms.

The early Middle Ages in the Latin-speaking West (the ninth to twelfth centuries) had no immediate approach to the ancient Greek philosophy. Augustine (354-430), a main source of mediaeval Platonism, learned Plato through Plotinus in the Latin translation of Victorinus, distinguished teacher of rhetoric at Rome and recent convert to Christianity. Both Plato and Aristotle appeared in the interpretations of the Greek and Latin neo-Platonists, who, like the Arabs, made one blend of traditional Greek philosophy. Aristotle, Plato's equally eminent pupil, has been called "the greatest of Platonists."[1]

Neo-Platonism had its rise in the world center of religion, Alexandria. Ammonius Saccas (Ammon: sack bearer, porter), father of neo-Platonism, was born of Christian parents; but according to McGiffert, translator of the *Church History* of Eusebius, his later teachings are not in accord with Christian theory (p. 265 n. 2; p. 267 n. 16). Ammonius was teacher in philosophy to the pagan Plotinus and the Christian Origen, who learned his theology from Clement of Alexandria, the elder contemporary of Ammonius.

Clement was a pupil of the Stoic convert Pantaenus, whom he followed as head of the Christian catechetical school of Alexandria (*ca.* 190–202). Origen succeeded Clement in the school.[2]

---

[1] E. S. Brightman, "Platonism," in Vergilius Ferm (ed.), *An Encyclopedia of Religion*, 593.

[2] Clement, *ca.* 150–213 ff.
Ammonius, 175–243.
Origen, *ca.* 185–254; head of school, *ca.* 211–32; in Caesarea, 232 ff.
Plotinus, 205?–70; teacher at Rome, 224.

Beginning with Ammonius the aim of neo-Platonism was to tie in Plato and Aristotle, and to keep the mystery which clings universally to the name of Plato.

The new system is founded on the *Enneads of Plotinus.* (Ammonius wrote no books.) As in Plato, all things come from God and return to God. From the One descends a series of emanations (the old Ideas of Plato): first, Intellect (*Nous*), both Mind and Being (Over-Mind); second, the World Soul (Over-Soul of the material cosmos). To Plato God is the first of the Ideas. To Plotinus the Ideas descend from the first divine emanation. Dean Inge takes *Spirit* to be the best word for the Greek *Nous.*[3]

The Alexandrine Philo, orthodox Jew and Hellenist philosopher (30/20 B.C.—A.D. 40/50), supplied the Greek Christian scholars of Alexandria with an allegorical method for the interpretation of Scripture. Philo believes that "reason is double both in the universe and also in the nature of mankind." There is the reason concerned with the incorporeal species, the patterns of the intellectual world, and the reason concerned with the visible objects of sight, the earthly copies of those invisible creations. (*Life of Moses* III.13.1, tr. Yonge.)

Dionysius the Areopagite, Paul's convert in Acts 17:34, is the pseudonymous author of a body of neo-Platonic writings from the end of the fifth century or the beginning of the sixth. Proclus (411-485), born in Constantinople, a teacher in Athens (*ca.* 450), who brought the philosophy into a system, is the immediate source. The Corpus Areopagiticum, or Corpus Dionysiacum, became a prime text in Christian theological studies, second only to the *Four Books of Sentences* of Peter Lombard (*ca.* 1100–1160/64)—a compilation of answers to dogmatic questions citing scriptural and patristic authority, preponderantly the Latin Fathers, with emphasis on Augustine.

Thomas Aquinas, as teacher of theology in the Dominican Studium at Paris, laid the foundation for his *Summa Theologica* with the exposition of the *Sentences* (1251/52). The Franciscan Bonaventure, whose *Commentary on the Sentences* is adjudged

[3] W. R. Inge, *The Philosophy of Plotinus,* II, viii.

his greatest work, was invested with the degree of Doctor of Theology on the same day as Aquinas (October 23, 1257), by the recently chartered University of Paris (chartered *ca.* 1200).

Boethius (*ca.* 480–524/5), translating the *Categories* and *On Interpretation* from Greek into Latin, gave the West about all it knew of the logic of Aristotle. More Platonist than Aristotelian, Boethius used and supplied a translation of Porphyry's *Isagogue,* the Introduction to the *Categories* of Aristotle. Porphyry the Syrian (232?–304?), teacher in Rome, editor and biographer of Plotinus, continued the tradition of Platonism.

The most famous of Boethius' original works was *The Consolation of Philosophy,* written in prison at Pavia in the brief period before the Ostrogoth emperor Theodoric the Great had the eminent statesman and philosopher executed, without a trial, as a traitor. Alfred, king of Wessex (871–99), labored at translating the *Consolation* from Latin into the old classic West Saxon. Chaucer's works contain a translation in the Midland dialect of fourteenth-century London and of Wycliff's Bible.

The Goths were early converts to Arian Christianity. Theodoric (king, 474–526) was educated at Constantinople, where he passed his youth as a hostage. Ulfilas, missionary to the Goths, was consecrated bishop at Constantinople in 341 by Eusebius of Nicomedia, who led the Arian party at the Council of Nicaea in 325. Ulfilas' incomplete translation of the Bible, the oldest literary monument in German, omitted the Books of the Kings because he felt that his constituency required no incitement to war.

Charlemagne called Alcuin from the cathedral school at York with a number of his scholars (782) to head the palace school at Aachen (the school moved with the court) and to rebuild the lapsed education in his extended domains.

Charles II (the Bald), Charles I of France, successor to the Empire, summoned the Irish scholar John Scotus Eri(u)gena to Paris (*ca.* 840–47) to head the palace school. Erigena translated Dionysius from Greek into Latin (*ca.* 850), and also parts of Maximus' commentaries on Dionysius. Erigena was a power for Platonism. Gilson remarks (*History,* p. 113) that if the Latins had followed his lead from Dionysius and Maximus, a neo-Platonist philosophy would have continued to dominate Western Europe throughout the Middle Ages. Erigena's free position on faith and reason brought down the condemnation of two councils.

Maximus of Chrysopolis (Maximus the Confessor) was martyred by Constans II in 662. The tongue that uttered and the hand that wrote would serve no more for controversy. The Third Council of Constantinople (680–81) decided against Constans' monotheletism, and with Maximus that there are two wills in Christ.

Erigena's Eastern contemporary, Al Kindi of Basra at the head of the Persian Gulf and of Baghdad on the Tigris, is an Arab neo-Platonist and Sufi mystic. (Al Kindi, d. *ca.* 870; Erigena, *ca.* 800–877/80). Weber, in *The History of Indian Literature* (p. 263), notes that Al Kindi included in his encyclopedic writings much out of Indian astronomy and arithmetic. Al Kindi *On the Intellect* is presented as according to Plato and Aristotle. The mystic's name is associated with the *Theology of Aristotle,* widely accepted throughout the Middle Ages as authentic. The book is a compilation from the *Enneads of Plotinus,* books IV to VI, and appropriately concerned with the soul.

The *Theology* is also conjectured to be altogether a Christian work, written by a Syrian monk in the language of the land, translated by a Christian Arab into Arabic (*ca.* 840), then into Latin by a Dominican.[4]

Somewhat later than Al Kindi and John Scotus Erigena is the name of the head of the Academy (Yeshivah) of Sura, Babylonia —the Egyptian-born Saadiah Gaon (882–942)—His Eminence Saadiah ben Joseph al-Fayyumi. The *Creeds and Dogmas*—the variously translated *Emunot ve Deot*—was written in Arabic. As Philo in the first century harmonized Greek and Hebrew thought, so Saadiah in the tenth effected a blend of Greek-Arabic and Jewish philosophy.

Saadiah translated the Hebrew Bible into Arabic for Moslems as well as Jews. The Jews turned the Arabic alphabet into the

---

4 Etienne Gilson, *A History of Christian Philosophy in the Middle Ages,* p. 637*n*2.

accustomed Hebrew characters. Besides the Pentateuch, which is still in use, one prophet, Isaiah, and half a dozen of the Writings are left. The largest part of his commentaries on the books of the Bible is gone. Like the Targums, the vernacular Aramaic interpretations that accompanied the reading of the Scriptures in the synagogue, Saadiah paraphrased the lively human attributions of God in rationalistic terms.

The Academy of Sura was founded in the third century. Saadiah was the only foreigner to attain the position of Gaon in either Sura or the rival academy of Pumbeditha.

The rabbinic interpreters in the Mishnah, "the Repetition" of the Law, are the tannaim. The commentators on the Mishnah are the amoraim. The Mishnah and the supercommentary, the Gemarah, make up the Talmud—"the Learning." The saboraim fill the interval before the Gaonim (Geonim), who exercise authority in all religious and legal questions for the entire Dispersion.

Saadiah had successfully challenged the prerogative of the Palestinian authorities to determine the incidence of the holy days. While still living in Egypt the youthful Saadiah seems to have opened his crusade against the Karaites (905/15).

Anan ben David, founder of Karaism in the eighth century, belonged to the ruling Davidic family of the Exile—a proper candidate for the office of civil head of the community, with the occasional privilege of appointing the Gaon, who was usually elected by the Academy. Saadiah was appointed to the gaonate of Sura by the exilarch, David ben Zakkai, who later excommunicated and exiled him to Baghdad. The Gaon answered by replacing the exilarch as he himself had been replaced. In the years of exile Saadiah wrote the *Creeds and Dogmas*. Friends restored peace between the religious and the civil head of Sura, and Saadiah resumed his place, which he held for the rest of his life (937–42). The exilarch died in 940 and Saadiah took the grandson of his old enemy to live with him and cared for him with fatherly solicitude.

The Karaites rejected oral tradition and separated themselves from the synagogue. Their ten articles of belief are stated by Judah Hadasi (1150), differing from other statements mainly in the matter that caused the division—"God has given to us the Torah, which is true and complete in every respect"—not wanting the addition of the so-called Oral Law; concurring in what all subscribe "that the Torah must be studied by every Jew in the original [Hebrew] language: that the Holy Temple was a place elected by God for His manifestation: that there is punishment and reward after death." These protestants also reaffirmed their belief in the resurrection of the dead and the coming of the Messiah, the son of David.[5]

Justinian closed the schools of philosophy in Athens in 529. The deposed scholars moved into Syria, Edessa on the upper Euphrates, and into Persia. The caliphs of Baghdad (762–1258) invited the Syrian scholars to the capital. They transmitted the Greek sciences and philosophy to the Arabic from the Syriac or immediately from the original Greek. (Greek was the language of the New Testament.) A familiar name in the West was the Nestorian Christian translator Hunain ibn Ishak (Johannitius). Hunain compiled for popular reading the *Dicta of the Philosophers* —the best from the Greek.

A common worship of Aristotle drew together Moslems, Jews, Catholics, to the mystic Arab philosophy. Al Farabi from Turkestan (870–950), Moslem mystic (Sufi), heads the list— the "distinguished scholar" whom Maimonides thought alone necessary to the study of Aristotle's logic. Avicenna (980–1037) from Bukhara in the Hindu Kush mountains, central home of the Aryan and the proto-European stock—Avicenna, most widely famed of Arab physicians, shares his pre-eminence in philosophy with Averroës of Cordova (1126–98), judge as well as physician and philosopher.

The mystic Al Ghazali of Khorasan (1059–1111), teacher in Nishapur, where his contemporary Omar the Tentmaker, the astronomer (d. *ca.* 1123), wrote the quatrains of the *Rubáiyát*; later teacher in Baghdad—Al Ghazali is the theologian of Islam.

---

[5] Solomon Schechter, *Studies in Judaism*, I, 160.

He parallels Maimonides and Thomas Aquinas in doctrinal authority. The exposition of the faith of Islam, confirmed in Al Ghazali's retreat in the Syrian desert, is contained in the *Revival of the Religious Sciences.*

In the twelfth century the four treatises that complete Aristotle's Logic—the *Organon* (The Instrument)—were discovered in Boethius' translation. Peter Abelard (1079–1142), who brought together the extreme positions of Realism and Nominalism with his mediating doctrine of Conceptualism and came nearest to Aristotle, had at hand only the *Categories* and the *Interpretation.* (The Universals—the Ideas—exist [Plato], but not outside their immediate forms of existence [Aristotle], except as in the mind of God before coming into being.)

The twelfth century was to bring to the Schoolmen the translations and the commentaries from Greek, Arab, and Jewish scholars. Under the authority of Bishop Raymond of Toledo and his successor in the bureau of translation in 1151, Archbishop John, many works were there brought over from Arabic into Latin. The head of the bureau, Dominicus Gundissalinus, working probably under Archbishop John, had among his helpers in translation a John of Spain (generally hyphenated with ibn Daud), who signed himself "the Israelite philosopher." The contemporary Abraham ibn Daud (*ca.* 1090–1160 ff.) was first among the Jews to give Aristotle the pre-eminence. In the company there was also "the Jew Solomon."

Among the works translated at Toledo was the *Fons Vitae* of Avicebrón (1021—58 ff.), which, read by the Schoolmen in Latin, was accepted as the work of a Moslem doctor, and later as a Christian Scholastic's. But Abu Ayyub Sulaiman ibn Yahya ibn Jabirul was "the Jewish Plato," the rabbi Solomon ben Judah ibn Gabirol. *The Fount of Life* ("For with thee is the fountain of life: in thy light shall we see light" [Psalm 36:9]) revived the old dispute on matter and form: Duns Scotus, the Franciscan, agreeing with Plato and Gabirol; the Domincans Albertus Magnus and Thomas Aquinas denying with Aristotle materiality to spiritual substances.

The Italian Anselm, Abbot of Bec, France (1078–93), Archbishop of Canterbury (1093–1109), was committed to the Augustinian tradition on the supereminence of faith, the free will of man, and the free grace of Heaven. ("Our darkness displeased us, we turned unto Thee, and there was light" [*Confessions* 13. 13].)

A moderate Realist (Plato moderated by Aristotle), Anselm was opposed by the extreme Nominalism (Aristotle) of Roscellinus (d. 1109/20). Peter Abelard battled both his teachers— Roscellinus and William of Champeaux, a Realist, head of the cathedral school of Paris.

The thirteenth-century Schoolmen bear characteristic titles. Alexander of Hales (d. 1245), the Irrefragable Doctor whose work is the basis of the first of many summae of religious philosophy, had Aristotle and the Arab commentaries.

Albert "the Great," the "Universal Doctor" (*ca.* 1206–80), took frequent note of the recently opened Arabic sources. Thomas Aquinas (1225–74), the "Angelic Doctor," is, like his teacher Albert, an Aristotelian. His *Summa Theologica* remains the authoritative statement of Catholic doctrine. Like his teacher, Aquinas is familiar with the current Jewish writings. After Aquinas' death, Albert, who had predicted the greatness of his protégé, went to Paris to defend his writings against the charge of being too favorable to the infidel philosophers. The Franciscan Bonaventure (1221–74), the mystic who leans to Plato and quotes Aristotle freely, the friend of Aquinas, is the "Seraphic Doctor."

John Duns Scotus (*ca.* 1265–1308), the Franciscan, the "Subtle Doctor," is a Platonist. The Thomists competed against the Scotists: the Dominicans against the Franciscans.

Aquinas has been classified as an Aristotelian Realist and Scotus as a Platonic Realist. Paul compasses the idealism of both Plato and Aristotle when he expresses his belief that the eternal counterpart is safe with God and that only the spirit can pass the tract of time (II Cor. 5:1; I Cor. 15:44–50).

The Franciscan Roger Bacon (*ca.* 1214–94), the "Admirable Doctor," is *the* scientist among the thirteenth-century Schoolmen.

William of Occam (d. 1349?), a Franciscan, the "Invincible Doctor," last in the great tradition of Scholasticism, returns to the Nominalist position that had been unpopular since Roscellinus' misadventure with Aristotle.

* * *

Philo the Jew, whose exegesis of Scripture was full of Platonic and Stoic elements, wrote his works in Greek, and he was, for the first Christian theologians of Alexandria, just about what Moses Maimonides was to be later on to the scholastic theologians of the thirteenth century: a model to imitate and, if possible, to excel. (Gilson, *History*, p. 29)

Mosheh ben Maimon (1135–1204), whose Arabic name is Abu Imran Musa ben Maimun ibn Abdallah, learned Aristotle of the Moslems among whom he lived all his life. If the fanaticism of the conquering Almohades drove him from his native Cordova (1148), the tolerance of the Egyptian Moslems allowed him to be court physician to Saladin and to write in peace his *Guide for the Perplexed* that the Moslems were to read in Arabic (the *Dalalat al-haïrin*), the Schoolmen in Latin (the *Dux* or *Director Neutrorum*), and the Jews in Hebrew (the *Moreh Nebuchim*).

Maimonides wrote the *Guide* (1180–90) to confirm by philosophy (Aristotle) the principles of revelation and tradition which he had expounded in the codification of the Talmud, the *Mishneh Torah* (the *Yad ha-Hazaka*—the Mighty Hand) at which he had labored in the years 1170–80, also in Egypt. This book was fated not to be called by its name, which was appropriated to the fifth book of the Law (*Deut.* 17:18). Like all his books except the *Misheh Torah*, which was written in Hebrew, the *Guide* was in Arabic.

The rabbi Samuel ibn Tibbon had the indorsement of the author and the advantage of consultation with him in putting the *Guide* into Hebrew. Most European languages follow Tibbon's literal version. The first Latin translation was based on the freer, more elegant Hebrew version of Jehudah al-Harizi. A Latin translation of the *Guide* in the Munich Library is identified with this version and credited to the joint effort of Jewish and Christian scholars at the court of Frederick II. The only complete Babylonian Talmud (completed in 1369) is also in the Munich Library (Heb. ms. No. 95).

Maimonides set no bounds to his admiration for Aristotle, except the Prophets. "The thorough understanding of Aristotle is the highest achievement to which man can attain, with the sole exception of the understanding of the Prophets."

The Moslems, the Christians, and the Jews, for all their devotion to Aristotle, were not able to follow him in his doctrine of the eternity of the universe, which Maimonides explains to his former pupil to whom he dedicates the *Guide* (Intro., p. 1): "In the name of God, Lord of the Universe: To R. Joseph (may God protect him!) son of R. Jehudah (may his repose be in Paradise!)."

Maimonides bases his argument for the being of a God on the philosophers' theory of the eternity of the universe (*Guide,* pp. 111 ff.) because this argument is logical and unshakable. The Prime Unmoved Mover of Aristotle can be only one, neither corporeal nor inhabiting a body. Having established on incontrovertible grounds the being of a God, Maimonides proceeds to prove the theory of creation as preferable to the eternity of the world "which Aristotle could not have considered conclusive 'after having himself taught us the rules of logic and the means by which arguments can be refuted or confirmed.' " Maimonides quotes Alexander of Aphrodisias in Caria, who lectured on Aristotelian philosophy in Athens (*ca.* A.D. 200).

Nachmanides blames Maimonides for following "that Greek Aristotle" while himself drawing on remote Platonic springs through the mazes of the Jewish theosophy, the Kabbala (the Tradition).

Rabbi Moses ben Nachman (Bonastruc de Portas), Nachmanides (*ca.* 1195—*ca.* 1270), lived quietly in the small town of Gerona, in the northern province of Catalonia, bordering on France. He earned his living as a physician. Doctor Schechter remarks (I, 102) that his calling as rabbi and teacher in Gerona, and later in Barcelona, meant the same as if it were said of a man that his profession was philanthropy.

Nachmanides, whose sympathies were with the conservative French rabbis, was drawn into the violent controversy about Maimonides' *Guide for the Perplexed* and the first book of his codification of the Law, the *Mishneh Torah,* setting forth his rule of exposition. To the French Jews, Nachmanides explained that the *Guide* was addressed to those misled by Aristotle and Galen, and that the code was strict about the prohibitions of the Law.

The loudest accuser of Maimonides was the Rabbi Solomon ben Abraham of Montpellier. He found at home a neglect of the study of the Law and the practice of the precepts. Some of the followers of Maimonides accused him in turn of denouncing the *Guide* and the code to the Inquisition in Provence (*ca.* 1234) —". . . playing with fire," says George Foot Moore in his *History of Religions* (II, 94). The books were publicly burned: Maimonides had died thirty years before in Egypt, widely acclaimed for his scholarly achievements.

The objections to Maimonides were that he placed philosophy too high, that he rationalized all the human symbols of God, that he carried allegory too far, explaining away all the miracles. The future life, the individual soul, the resurrection, no longer bear the sureness of faith. The angels are the meditating intelligences whom Aristotle interposes between the Prime Unmoved Mover and the moving spheres.

Nachmanides in his *Commentary on the Pentateuch* is the authoritative spokesman for the conservative opposition. Judaism is based on the belief in miracles, the creation from nothing, the omniscience of God, the divine Providence.

Fra Pablo Christiani, the converted Jew, confident that he can demonstrate the messiahship of Jesus out of the Talmud and the rabbis, challenges Nachmanides to a debate and wins an order from the king, James I of Aragón, for the meeting, which takes place in Barcelona July 21 to July 24 or 25, 1263, before the king, the court, and prominent ecclesiastics.

Doctor Schechter remarks that it was the same Talmud that was burned in Paris some twenty years before at the instance of another Jewish convert for anti-Christian passages (I, 104). This first public disputation between Jews and Christians inspired by the zeal of the convert Nicholas Donin resulted in the bull *Impia Gens* in the same year (1244) and in the censorship that took old Rabbi Talmus to the stake so often. Albert in Paris, teaching at the university (1240/45–48), was invited by Pope Innocent IV to sit at a conference on the Talmud. The ancient rabbinic compilation of commentary and supercommentary on the Hebrew Bible was not unfamiliar to Albertus Magnus.

The questions in debate between Nachmanides and Pablo were—

Had the Messiah appeared?

Was the Messiah announced by the prophets divine or of human father and mother?

Where the Jews or the Christians in possession of the true faith?

Nachmanides answered that the Jew is bound to believe in the truth of the Bible. The Talmud gives the interpretations of rabbis. To the prophets the Messiah was a man: the Messianic Kingdom of peace and justice had not yet come. The world was still full of violence and injustice, and the Christians were the most warlike.

On the fourth day both sides were ready to conclude the debate, but the king wished it to continue. He granted Nachmanides' request for immunity and at the close gave him a purse in appreciation.

The Dominicans felt they had won. Nachmanides published the argument and was charged with blasphemy. The king had the hearing held in his presence. The commission sympathized with Nachmanides; still, the pamphlet was ordered to be burned. A fine was remitted to Nachmanides' brother. An appeal to Pope Clement IV by the Dominicans extended the sentence from two years of banishment to perpetual exile. Clement in July, 1267, issued the Bull *Turbato Corde* (With a disturbed heart), authorizing the Inquisition in Spain to proceed against apostate Jews and Judaizers.

In 1267 Nachmanides is in Palestine. He writes home of

the desolation left by the Mongol invasion. It is hard to gather the ten men required for a synagogue service.

Nachmanides settled in Acre. There he wrote his *Commentary on the Pentateuch,* gathered disciples, and exerted a wide influence in his public lectures.

The longing for his home and his family finds no consolation except to weep over the ruins of the Temple. He writes to his boys minute instructions on guarding their souls in purity and humility. The son who stands before the king (of Castile) is admonished never to do anything which his father would disapprove. He is also to remind himself with the Psalmist: "I am a stranger in the earth" (Psalm 119:19).

Nachmanides, whose last years were given to the spiritual upbuilding of the Holy Land, was struck down by a native, so the story goes, as he approached the ancestral site, chanting his hymn to Zion.

THE INQUISITION

CAESAR'S INQUISITION

THE Inquisition came into the Church with Caesar. Before Constantine adopted the Christian symbol a vast empire counted its most dangerous enemies those who professed their Christian faith. Ignatius Theophorus (God-clad, God-bearing) Bishop of Antioch in Syria, was on his way to "enter the contest" in the Roman arena (Tradition has it in the time of Trajan about 106 or 107) when he wrote his *Seven Letters to the Churches.*

Eusebius' *Ecclesiastical History* (book III, chapter 33) quotes the Greek translation of Tertullian's *Apology,* where Tertullian represents Pliny and Trajan as inclined to be lenient toward the Christians. Pliny the Younger inquires of his friend Trajan how to deal with these Christians. His practice has been to ask three times if they were Christians. If three times they answered yes, he ordered them executed—such "pertinacious and inflexible obstinacy" deserved punishment.[1]

The parable of the Tares and the Wheat (Wait till the harvest) serves as guide to the Christian Fathers: the Church should not for any cause shed blood.

Tertullian, father of Latin theology, defender of the faith against heretic and pagan, says in brief: "It is not religious [not of religion] to force religion." (*"Sed nec religionis est religionem colere."*) (*Tertullian adversus Scapulam,* ch. II; *ca.* A.D. 211–12.)

---

[1] Eusebius, *Church History,* p. 165*n*1 (III.33); also Josephus, *Antiquities of the Jews,* II, 604 (appendix).

The mild Lactantius, adviser to Constantine and tutor to the emperor's ill-fated eldest son, Crispus, had experienced the harshness of the state toward those who would not hail Caesar as divine —would not so much as take up a bit of incense and place it on the brazier before his image. Lactantius argues at length on the theme: "To defend religion a man must be willing to die, but not to kill." (*Institutes* V.20; A.D. 308.)

From the beginning, Gnosticism in all its forms was the most dreaded heresy in the Church (John 1; I John 1). The widespread cult, descended from the Persian Mani, had behind it all the dualistic oriental mysteries.

Priscillian, learned, eloquent, wealthy, ascetic, attracted to his oath-bound society the bishops Instantius and Salvianus. The Catholic bishop of Cordova, Hyginus, spoke his doubts on Priscillian to the bishops Ithacius and Idacius. The two bishops call the Synod of Saragossa (380), which is attended by the Spanish bishops and bishops from Aquitaine, across the Pyrennes. Priscillian and four of the leaders ignore the summons to appear and are excommunicated. In answer the rebels ordain Priscillian a priest and appoint him Bishop of Avila.

The unrelenting bishops appeal to Gratian, emperor of the West. Priscillian and his sympathizers are denied the use of churches and are sent into exile. Priscillian and his two companion bishops travel to Damasus at Rome and Ambrose in Milan and are coldly received, if at all.

An appeal to the imperial court brings a revocation of the sentence, and again Ithacius calls on the emperor. Gratian is assassinated in Paris and Maximus the usurper, anxious to appear orthodox, convokes the Synod of Bordeaux (384). Instantius is first tried and deposed and Priscillian appeals to Maximus at Trier. Martin of Tours, displeased that the case should be brought before a secular court, exacts the promise from Maximus that there will be no bloodshed. Priscillian and some others are found guilty of magic. The verdict goes to Maximus. Priscillian and "a number of his followers" are put to the sword: Priscillian had himself recommended this punishment for Manichaeans.

Now both Ithacius, who had pursued Priscillian to the death, and the emperor Maximus are denounced. Damasus and Ambrose add their censure. Martin returns to Tours and compels Maximus to recall the "military tribunal" already on the way to Spain to root out the heresy. Ithacius is deposed by a synod of Spanish bishops and Idacius is forced to resign.

The sympathy felt for Priscillian was dissipated as the sect grew and flourished. Synods were convoked in Spain by Pope Leo in 446 and 447, but the heresy did not decline. There was a secret community of Manichaeans in Rome which Pope Leo looked into with senators and presbyters in 443. Those who refused to adopt the orthodox faith were banished from Rome by the civil authorities. Leo is in the list of early churchmen who rejected the penalty of death for heresy, but as the sect of the Manichaeans penetrated into the civil and religious order, Leo was led to denounce the unnatural doctrines that would break down all laws, human and divine.[2]

---

[2] *Nicene and Post-Nicene Fathers,* 2d Series, XII, 20-26: Leo I (the Great), letter 15, to Turribius, Bishop of Asturias in northern Spain, A.D. 447.

THE EARLY EUROPEAN INQUISITION

THE early mediaeval scholars debated on philosophy with no likely hazard beyond the censure of a superior. The polemic writings of Alan of Lille (d. 1202) mark the change in the intellectual climate (Gilson, *History*, p. 172). There are dim references to the martyrdom of Roscelin (Roscellinus), the Breton canon (1050–1109/20), for being wrong on Aristotle and substituting the vocal word for the ultimate reality of the name.

Peter Abelard (1079–1142) wrote the *Sic et Non* (Thus and Not Thus; Yea and Nay), setting in juxtaposition the sentences of the Fathers. Bernard of Clairvaux, champion of orthodoxy, preacher of the Second Crusade (1147–49), brought about Abelard's second meeting with the bishops at Sens (1141). (The first meeting was at Soissons in 1121.) Still Bernard was no inquisitor. His rule was *Fides suadenda non imponenda* (Faith calls for persuasion, not imposition). Abelard's method became a model for the university Schoolmen of the twelfth century. Bernard engaged in open disputation at Mayence (November, 1146) with the monk Radulph, who was rousing the people of the Rhineland against the Jews.

Frederick I, Barbarossa, of the Hohenstaufen line, King of Germany in 1152, crowned emperor at Rome in 1155 by Pope Adrian IV (Nicholas Breakspear, the only English pope) — Frederick met Pope Lucius III at Verona (1184) and agreed that all heretics were to be sought out, brought before the bishop's court, excommunicated, and handed over to the civil power for due punishment.

Frederick felt himself to be in the line of Caesars and so entitled to rule Italy. The North was settled by the German Lombards (568). Henry VI, Frederick's son, married Constance, heir to Sicily and Naples. Frederick II, Barbarossa's grandson, was orphaned at the age of four and became ward and vassal of Pope Innocent III (1198), feudal lord of Naples and Sicily (the Two Sicilies). The Papal States occupied central Italy. They were donations of the pious, beginning with the gift of the exarchate of Ravenna to Pope Stephen II by Pepin, son of Charles Martel. The Papal States became independent of the Empire about 1200 under Pope Innocent III.

Pope Urban II proclaimed the First Crusade, approved by the Council of Clermont, fervently preached by Peter the Hermit, whose text was drawn from Jeremiah's Dooms of the Nations in which *The Prophet* breaks into the dirge meter as he laments the fate of Moab (see 48:36):

Therefore my heart for Moab like pipes moaneth,
And my heart for the men of Kir-heres like pipes moaneth.

Peter invokes the dramatic line: "Cursed be he that keepeth back his sword from blood" (48:10).

The First Crusade was a popular movement in which no king participated. It established the Latin kingdom at Jerusalem (1099–1143). After Raymond IV, Count of Toulouse, refused the crown, Godfrey of Bouillon, elected king, declined the title and called himself Protector of the Holy Sepulchre. His brother Baldwin succeeded him shortly and assumed the title of king.

The Second Crusade (1147–49) was preached after the fall of Edessa. Pope Eugenius III and Saint Bernard of Clairvaux urged Emperor Conrad III and Louis VII of France to lead the fruitless expedition.

The Third Crusade (1189–92), called by Pope Gregory VIII because Jerusalem had fallen to Saladin (1187), was led by a confederacy of kings: the Emperor Frederick Barbarossa, drowned on the way in the Kalykadnos River in Asia Minor, Philip Augustus of France, Richard I of England, and William of Sicily, besides the King of Hungary, Leopold of Austria, and the city of

Venice. The Fourth Crusade (1202–4) was turned against Constantinople, whose fall opened the way to the Ottoman Turks. The new Latin Empire lasted from 1205 to 1261.

There is a strange contrast between the capture of Jerusalem by the Moslems and the capture by the Christians. When the city fell to the Crusaders in 1099 not one inhabitant was spared. The Jews were burned in their synagogue. When Saladin took Jerusalem, as when Omar took it at the first in 636, no life was lost. Saladin set a fixed ransom that would avert the doom of slavery and allowed the sick and wounded a year's respite with the Knights Hospitalers to attend them.

Gregory I, the Great (590–604), in his letters established the principle of protection for the Jews. He forbade the use of force as long as the Jews kept within the limits set by the Church: the forced conversion of minors was also forbidden.

Calixtus II (*ca.* 1120) in the bull *Sicut Judaeis* (the words echo Gregory) follows the rule of Gregory in answer to the appeal of the Jews against the violence of the Crusaders on their way to the Holy Land (1096 ff.) with the war cry *Hierosolyma est perdita*: "Just as the Jews ought not to have the license to do . . . more than the law permits them, so ought they not suffer curtailment in those privileges which have been conceded them." Calixtus pronounced against the desecration of synagogues and cemeteries.

Innocent III (1198–1216) raised the Papacy to its height of power. Early in his reign Innocent reissued the bull of Calixtus. Innocent presided at the Fourth Lateran Council (1215), which imposed fresh restrictions on the Jews (one, the wearing of the badge) with the admonition: "They ought not to be excessively oppressed by believers, for they are the living witness of the true religion."

Innocent blamed the Jews for inciting the Albigenses to heresy. He ordered a crusade against the heretics in 1208. Simon de Montfort conducted a bloody campaign in the peaceable region of Languedoc, culminating in the victory at Muret (1213). Raymond VI, Count of Toulouse, supported the heretics and lost his lands, which he later regained from Simon de Montfort. Raymond IV of Toulouse brought an army to the First Crusade.

James I of Aragón (king from 1213 to 1276) asks for a bull of inquisition against the Albigenses. (James' father, Pedro II, died in the battle of Muret fighting for the Albigensian cause.) The request is refused by Gregory IX and his three immediate successors: Celestine IV, Innocent IV, and Alexander IV. By 1255 in Alexander's time the Inquisition reached over Europe.

Frederick II, the Great (1194–1250), issued his constitution for the Empire (1220) quoting the letter of Innocent III written in 1199 to the magistrates of Viterbo, a district in the Papal States: If treason against the state is a capital offense, and the children of those condemned are spared only through pity, how much greater is the offense against the Divine Majesty!

In the constitution for Lombardy (1224) Frederick decrees death for Manichaeans. Gregory IX entered this rescript among the Pontifical Epistles (1230/31): Heretics convicted by the Church were to be given over to the civil magistrates for due punishment—the same *animadversio debita* agreed to by Frederick I and Lucius III at Verona in 1184.

Gregory promulgated the bull *Etsi Judaeorum* in 1233 and again in 1235 commanding that the Christians treat the Jews as they themselves would hope to be treated in non-Christian lands.

Frederick protests sharply to the Abbot of Fulda over the blood accusation with its hideous accompaniments that occurred when the Crusaders were assembled about Fulda at Christmas time 1238. (Five sons of a miller were found slain.) Only the intercession of the magistrate and some of the citizens kept the small community from being entirely wiped out.

Innocent IV (1243–54), rigorous in the pursuit of heresy, promulgator of the bull *Ad Extirpanda* (1252), ordering the civil magistrates to execute within five days the penalty for heresy on those handed over by the ecclesiastical courts, and the bull *Impia Gens* (1244), ordering the burning of the Talmud, still issued and reissued the bull *Sicut Judaeis* and characterized the ritual blood accusation as a libel in any of its forms. The hostility to the Talmud was due to the belief that it kept the Jews from being Christians.

Frederick participated fully in the life of his age. The year of the second rescript he chartered the University of Naples in connection with the monastic school of Salerno, long famous for medicine. He had Jewish scholars at his court. He commissioned his astrologist, Michael Scott (d. 1235), to translate into Latin the Moslem philosophers Avicenna and Averroës. Frederick, reared in Sicily, had a strong bent toward the Moslem philosophy. While under the ban of excommunication, Frederick went on the unrecognized crusade of 1228–29. As ward and vassal of Innocent III he had vowed a crusade.

Frederick is hailed as a man ahead of his time and the organizer of a well-ordered modern state. Frederick opened the early European Inquisition and in 1224 allowed the tribunal in Sicily a third of the property confiscated from the Jews. The instrument of investigation served as well against political enemies. Later the Inquisition in Palermo assessed the Jews for the expenses of the court. Ferdinand and Isabella (Ferdinand II of Sicily in 1468) confirmed the earlier agreement on the division of the spoils when the Inquisition in Sicily came under the jurisdiction of Spain.

THE SPANISH INQUISITION

POPE GREGORY IX (1227–41) instituted an inquisition into errorists within the Church, appointing members of the new mendicant orders, Dominicans and Franciscans, to the work. He did not establish a separate court.

Ferdinand V of Castile, II of Aragón and Sicily, III of Naples, was proclaimed King of Sicily by his father, John II of Aragón and Navarre in 1468. Ferdinand and Isabella set up an inquisition in Sicily in 1477, antedating the infamous establishment in Spain. The New or Spanish Inquisition was directed first against the neo-Christians, the *conversos,* "Maranos,"[1] secondly against Jews and Moors.

Ferdinand, aflame with greed, was more easily convinced than Isabella that these new Christians had no intention of taking the adopted religion to heart. Maranos and professed Jews moved freely in the court of Ferdinand and Isabella. Ferdinand's mother, Juana Enríquez, second wife of Juan II of Aragón, daughter of the Admiral of Castile, Frederique Enríquez, was granddaughter of the beautiful Jewish Paloma of Toledo.

Maranos and Jews were happy to advance the marriage of Ferdinand and Isabella. Pedro (or Moysen) Caballeria, member of a large and prominent Marano family of Saragossa, was called upon to win ecclesiastical approval for the marriage. Isabella's parents preferred an alliance with France or Portugal.

Don Abraham Senior of Segovia, farmer of taxes for Castile, lent his house in Toledo for the courtship. In one account another of the faithless, with no pretense to conversion, Don Selemoh of

---

[1] In modern Spanish *marranos*—"swine."

Aragón, presents Ferdinand's gift to Isabella—a necklace of gold beads costing 40,000 ducats and bought with a loan from Ferdinand's "beloved friend," Yayme Ram, son of a rabbi and a prominent jurist. In the Caballeria story Pedro negotiates the marriage, presents Ferdinand's gift to Isabella, and pays for it in large part. Ferdinand and Isabella had each two Marano secretaries. Isabella's confessor, Fernando de Talavera, Archbishop of Granada, was of Jewish ancestry on his mother's side.

With what vain hope must the Marano Minister of the Budget, Don Luis de Santangel, have urged the support of Ferdinand and Isabella for Columbus' voyage of exploration. Even in the ample spaces divided between Spain and Portugal by the bull of Pope Alexander VI in 1493 and the Treaty of Tordesillas, Spain, in 1494 the persecuted from the homeland found no release. Alexander conferred the title "the Catholic" on Ferdinand and Isabella.

A series of outbursts against the Jews and the Moors, especially the widespread assaults in 1391, had driven many to capitulate.

The Moors were an integral part of Spain. In 711 they had settled in New Castile, south of Old Castile, when they superseded the West Gothic kingdom with its capital Toletum (418–711). Many of the native population moved north and began the Christian kingdoms of Asturias (León), Navarre, Castile, Aragón.

The Moors penetrated deep into France and were thrown back by Charles Martel at the Battle of Tours (or Poitiers) in 732. The terms Arab, Moslem, Moor, Saracen refer to geographic or historic circumstance. An Arab is a nomad out of the Syrian desert (Deut. 26:5). Moslem is the term of faith. The Moors are the dark men (Mauroi) living in Mauretania, North Africa. The Islamic peoples of Spain are called Moors. Saracen, a name given by the Romans to the Arab tribes on the Syrian border, relates specially to the Crusades.

The Spanish, the Western, Caliphate, an offshoot of the Omayyad Dynasty of Damascus, at first an emirate under Abd-er-Rahman, builder of the famous Mosque of Cordova, continued with

Cordova as its capital from 756 to 1236. The independent Omayyad Dynasty of Spain (to 1031) outlasted the parent dynasty of Damascus (660–750). The Moorish Caliphate, with its capital at Granada (1238–1492), was the second center of a brilliant civilization.

The Christian kingdom of Asturias, dating from the eighth century, merged with León in the tenth. Sancho III of Navarre (1001–35) took Castile from the Moors in 1028 and gave it to his second son, Ferdinand I, in 1033. Ferdinand conquered León and also became overlord of the Moslem cities—Toledo, Saragossa, Seville.

Alfonso VI of León, I of Castile, takes Toledo from the Moors, the second city of the Spanish Caliphate, in 1085. The Moorish outpost, Madrid, in New Castile, later favorite residence of Emperor Charles V, fell to Alfonso in 1083. The Almoravides from North Africa defeat Alfonso and settle in Spain (1086). Following them from North Africa the Almohades conquer the tolerant Almoravides and set up their kingdom (1147–1232). Jews and Christians are allowed to choose between Islam, emigration, and death. Maimonides, then thirteen years of age, leaves Spain with his family (1148).

Ferdinand III of Castile and León permanently unites the two kingdoms in 1230. He takes the capital of the Western Caliphate, Cordova, in 1236 and Seville in 1248.

November 1, 1478, Sixtus IV (Xystus: Zystus) signed, reluctantly, the bull so urgently pressed by Isabella's advisers, among them the Papal Nuncio, Niccolo Franco—the bull allowing Ferdinand and Isabella to choose archbishops, bishops, laymen to constitute a court of inquiry into the faith of their subjects. Sixtus had disallowed the canonization of the two-year-old Simon of Trent, the hero of a laboriously contrived blood accusation; however, he exculpated the participants in the bull of the same year (June 20, 1478): It was "fitly and rightly done."

Their Majesties are busied with the Moors. Early in September of 1480 Isabella signs, unwillingly, for Castile. At the end of September, 1480, two Dominicans—Juan de San Martín and

Miguel de Morillo—appear with their two aids. In January, 1481, the court sits at Triana, a suburb of Seville. February 6, 1481, Seville sees its first auto-da-fé.

The plot to resist with arms was discovered, and on this occasion six of the wealthiest Maranos (men and women) mounted the *quemadero,* the place of burning. On succeeding days the most prominent Maranos and great numbers who had fled to other cities, returned to Seville at the demand of the Inquisitors (enforced by the papal bull of April 3, 1481), their property confiscated, made up a rich harvest for the royal treasury. In the *Catholic Encyclopedia* the auto-da-fé is the act of faith (*actus fidei*), the solemn proceedings on the day when the errant are received again into the Church: in the *Jewish Encyclopedia* the auto-da-fé means the fires of the Inquisition.

January 29, 1482, Sixtus sends a brief to Ferdinand and Isabella protesting the conditions of inquiry. He would dismiss the inquisitors except for consideration of Their Majesties. Isabella writes to the Pope disapproving the absolution of condemned heretics. Sixtus answers in the autograph of January or February 23, 1483: "It seems to us that the Queen is urged to institute and confirm the Inquisition by ambition and a desire for worldly goods rather than by zeal for the faith and true fear of God."

Bulls and briefs do not restrain. Threats to remove the inquisitors are not carried out. The Popes try to mitigate the proceedings of the courts; but, the power once granted, the search is avidly pursued and the voice of admonition is weakened or defied.

Tomás de Torquemada (Turris-cremata: Torre quemada), aged sixty-three, prior of the Dominican monastery of Santa Cruz at Segovia, confessor to the Infanta Isabella in Segovia, counselor to the Queen (1474 ff.)—Torquemada is the first Grand Inquisitor of Spain. Torquemada, Inquisitor-General for Avignon, Valencia, Catalonia (October, 1481), is one of seven added to the inquisitional staff of Castile within two weeks of the brief of January 29, 1482 (February 11). In October, 1483, he becomes Inquisitor-General for Castile and Aragón.

As head of the Inquisition, Torquemada establishes courts, chooses inquisitors who are accountable to him, appoints a commission of five to assist him in hearing all appeals from the decisions of the tribunal. Because the Jews helped the Maranos and were themselves theoretically outside the jurisdiction of the courts, Torquemada urged Ferdinand and Isabella to force the Jews to become Christians or to leave Spain.

Among the aids of Torquemada the names of Lucero, inquisitor of Cordova; Arbues of Saragossa in Aragón; Deza, successor to Torquemada as Inquisitor-General, stand out and set the character of the Inquisition.

Torquemada presided at Seville from 1483 to 1498. The second court was established at Cordova. Diego Rodríguez Lucero, most faithful henchman of Diego Deza, was grandly rewarded by Ferdinand and Isabella for his success in tracing any hint of a Jewish connection in or out of the Church. He pursued the Archbishop of Granada, confessor to Isabella, as a Marano.

The young Bachelor of Divinity, Membreque, preached on Jewish doctrines to his congregation of one hundred and seven. Lucero obtained a list of those present and every person was burned alive. Ferdinand was compelled to dismiss Deza. The Supreme Council of the Inquisition with Cardinal Ximenes, third of the Grand Inquisitors, sent Lucero in chains to the castle of Burgos in May, 1508. The Catholic Congregation, composed of the highest ecclesiastics of Spain, meeting at Valladolid in August, 1508, orders all in prison on the charge of Judaizing to be freed.

Pedro Arbues, Augustinian canon in Saragossa, and the Dominican Gaspar Juglar were appointed inquisitors for Aragón by Torquemada. The violent opposition in the Cortes, whose consent was necessary, delayed the institution in Aragón until April, 1484. The first auto-da-fé took place in Saragossa May 10. The *Jewish Encyclopedia* reports two autos-da-fé in the first month of office, with no further record of trials. Arbues was assassinated in September, 1485. The intercession of the young Archbishop de Aragón prevented a massacre.

In the conspiracy was Alfonso de la Caballeria, vice-chancellor of Aragón, whom the Pope and Ferdinand defended against a charge of Judaizing heresy, although he had not severed his connection with a large synagogue in Saragossa. Only one of the nine brothers, Benveniste, had refused to follow the lead of the eldest, Bonafos. Benveniste's son and his son's wife became Christians, and his daughter married a Marano, a large landholder of Verdun. A son of Alfonso married a granddaughter of the king.

Bonafos on his conversion in 1450 took the name Pedro (Micer): one of his brothers (Samuel) took the same name. Bonafos was a scholar of Hebrew, Greek, Latin, and learned in civil and canonical law. He spent the years from 1450 to his violent death in 1464 writing a book against Jews and Moslems (*Zelus Christi Contra Judaios et Sarracenos*). Jaime, son of Bonafos, accompanied Ferdinand to Naples. A trusted counselor to the king, he still fell victim to the Inquisition in 1504.

Francisco Ximenes (Jiménez) de Cisneros (1436–1517)— priest, soldier, statesman, patron of scholars, philanthropist—joined in 1484 the strict Franciscan Observantine Congregation in the Friary of St. John at Toledo. Appointed confessor to Isabella in the fateful year 1492, the simple monk continued to live the cloistered life. In 1495 Ximenes became Archbishop of Toledo and Primate of Spain: in 1507 Cardinal and Inquisitor-General. In 1509 he leads the assault on Oran. In the interval between the death of Ferdinand (1516) and Charles' succession Ximenes is regent of Spain. The following year Charles relieves him of his state offices.

Ximenes founded the new University of Alcalá de Henares in the town of that name, twenty miles east of Madrid. Here the cardinal assembled scholars to compile at his expense the Complutensian Polyglot Bible (Complutum the name of the old Roman town). The six volumes presented the parallel Old Testament texts in Hebrew, Greek, Vulgate Latin, the Aramaic Pentateuch (the Targum of Onkelos with a Latin translation), and the Greek New Testament with a Latin translation. Three Marano scholars are prominently named—Alfonso of Zamora, Alfonso of Alcalá, Paul Núñez of Segovia. Erasmus used the compilation to advantage in the fourth edition (1527) of his Greek-Latin New Testament, especially in the book of Revelation.

In the third century Origen at Caesarea had labored to bring about a standard Greek Old Testament to match the Hebrew Old Testament done by the scribes at Tiberias in the second century. Like Ximenes, Origen set in the first column of his Hexapla Bible (six columns, eight in prophecy and poetry) the "Text of the Sopherim." Origen, the most prolific of the Church writers, is said to have employed fourteen male stenographers and seven female calligraphers.

With Ximenes we see the Conquistadores in a new light. When the lay colonist Bartolomé de Las Casas of Hispaniola, ordained a priest in 1510, visits Spain on behalf of the enslaved native population (1515), the cardinal appoints him "Protector of the Indians." Later as a Dominican Las Casas has the support of the brothers in his labors. The missionary to the Indians was also their historian.

Ximenes was a mild inquisitor until he learned that Charles on the advice of his Flemish counselors was inclined to accept a huge bribe to moderate the Inquisition. Ximenes built a palace at Alcalá where the state records were kept. There, "admirably arranged," were to be read the names and crimes of those who met the judgment of the Inquisition.

In 1496 Joanna, daughter of Ferdinand and Isabella, heiress to the Spanish domains, married Philip I (the Handsome), son of Emperor Maximilian I and Mary of Burgundy, daughter of Charles the Bold—Mary's dower the Netherlands and the rich country of fluid borders dividing France from Germany and the Empire. Mary died in 1482 and her infant son, Philip I, succeeded to the throne of the Netherlands. The Duchy of Burgundy reverted to France on the death of Charles (1477) the year of Mary's marriage. (John, heir apparent, only son of Ferdinand and Isabella, married to Margaret, daughter of Maximilian, died in 1497.)

The house of Hapsburg arose in the German-speaking Swiss canton Aargau and was named from its ancestral home, the Hawk's Castle. Rudolf I, successor to his father, Count Albert IV of Hapsburg, was elected King of Germany and Emperor of the Holy Roman Empire (1273–91).

Isabella dies in 1504. The Maranos appeal to Joanna and

Philip in Flanders. They order Deza to halt the Inquisition (September 30, 1505) until their arrival in Spain. Joanna goes mad at the sudden death of her husband in 1506 and Ferdinand acts as regent. The Santa Junta, the desperate "League for Liberty," has the mad Joanna as captive patron (1520–21).

The two sons of Joanna and Philip, Charles I, King of Spain in 1516, elected emperor as Charles V in 1519, crowned at Aachen (Aix-la-Chapelle) the next year, and his younger brother, Ferdinand I, divide the vast territories assembled by their grandparents—Ferdinand and Maximilian. (It is interesting to note that Francis I of France and Henry VIII of England were contenders for the imperial title.)

Ferdinand, founder of the new Austrian branch of the Hapsburgs, holds Austria, Hungary, Bohemia. He married Princess Anna of Hungary in 1521, and on the death of Anna's brother, Louis II, in 1526 was elected to the throne of Bohemia and Hungary, which now came under Hapsburg rule. Charles gave up all his powers but not his worldly interests when he retired to the monastery of St. Jerome in Yuste, Spain, in 1556. Charles' son, Philip II, received the Netherlands and Spain with its dependencies. Ferdinand received Germany and the imperial title, which continued in the Austrian branch of the Hapsburgs.

The dynasty of Hapsburg, the oldest reigning family in Europe, passed in our time—the immediate occasion the assassination of the Archduke Francis Ferdinand (heir to the throne of Austria-Hungary) while riding in procession through Sarajevo, Bosnia, with his wife on June 28, 1914. Franz Joseph's son, the gifted and sensitive Rudolf, had fallen victim to a romantic adventure twenty-five years before.

The restive, alien populations had strong ties of religion, language, nationality to Serbia, whose independence of the Ottoman overlord was recognized by the Congress of Berlin (1878), which allowed Austria to occupy Bosnia-Herzegovina. In 1908 Austria annexed the province. The rejection by Serbia of the ultimatum of Austria, backed by the German emperor, William II, whose path to the East was blocked by Serbia, quickly drew in the allies on both sides.

The aged Franz Joseph, symbol of despotism and reaction, whose reign (1848–1916) began in insurrection, whose career was the summation of tragedy (the Empress Elizabeth, traveling incognito, died by the knife of an anarchist as she boarded a lake steamer at Geneva in 1898)—Francis Joseph lived to see his empire crumble in the tumult of a world at war.

THE PORTUGUESE INQUISITION

PORTUGAL and Spain have a common historic background and almost a common history. Alfonso I, first King of Portugal (1139–85), son of Henry of Burgundy, Count of Portugal, married a daughter of Alfonso VI of León and Castile. Alfonso I established the Order of Aviz for defense against the Moors. John I, the Great (1385–1433), Grand Master of the military-religious order (1364), founder of the dynasty, receives refugees from the violent disorders of 1391 in Spain. The House of Aviz ruled Portugal in the great days of maritime enterprise. Prince Henry the Navigator, third of the six sons of John, promoter of seafaring and commerce, forbade the kidnapping of Negroes for the slave trade from the newly explored West African coast (1455).

After the interval of Spanish rule (1580–1640) John IV, Duke of Braganza, a descendant of John I and Emanuel of the House of Aviz, begins the new line. John II, proceeding against the nobles, had executed the Duke of Braganza in Lisbon (1483). On this occasion the king's treasurer, Isaac Abravanel, departed for Toledo.

The "mild and gentle Affonso V" appointed Dom Judah Abravanel treasurer and minister of finance, and called his counselor Joseph ben David ibn Yahya (John) his "wise Jew."

John II (1481–95), son of Alfonso, extended a provisional hospitality to thousands of Jews expelled from Spain in 1492. He offered a permanent residence to six hundred families for a payment of sixty thousand cruzados. (The cruzado was roughly half a dollar.) A number of metalworkers and armorers were free to remain. The rest were to depart in eight months for Africa in vessels provided by the king. Those who overstayed their leave would be sold as slaves.

Isabel writes to Emanuel (1495–1521), cousin and brother-in-law of John II: If he will refuse admission to the Jews from Spain and will expel the Jews from Portugal he may marry her daughter. Emanuel cherished the ambition of uniting all the kingdoms of the Iberian Peninsula. He consults the Council of State, which is averse to losing "such a useful and diligent people" who will then settle in Africa and help the Moslems.

Isabella, young widow of the Infante of Portugal, herself writes to Emanuel. She would not enter Portugal until it was cleared of Jews. The marriage contract is signed November 30, 1496. The edict of December 4, 1496, commands all Jews to leave Portugal by the end of October, 1497. Any Christian concealing a Jew after that date will have his property confiscated. No future ruler is to allow Jews to reside in Portugal. An amnesty of twenty years is granted to the Maranos on May 30, 1497. April 20, 1499, they are forbidden to leave without the king's permission. Isabella dies in 1498 and Emanuel marries her sister, Mary, who becomes the mother of John III and Isabella of Portugal. Emanuel's third wife, Leonora of Austria, was a sister of Charles. Charles married John's sister Isabella, and John married Charles' sister Catherine.

On the advice of a *converso*, Levi ben Shem Tob, all the children from the age of three to nineteen are to be baptized and become wards of the king. The Jews are informed of the plan on March 17, 1497, and Sunday, the first day of the Passover, March 19, the plan is put into general execution. (Many Christians hide Jewish children.) The Bishop Fernando Coutinho bears testimony to the appalling scenes at the forcible conversion when parents killed their children and themselves, calling the All-Knowing to witness that they chose to die in the Mosaic faith. Shortly before the limit for departure, all were ordered to leave from Lisbon. About twenty thousand were there when they were told the time had expired and they were the king's slaves. The majority yielded to this militant evangelism. Some escaped to Italy, Africa, Turkey.

Isabella had obtained a promise from Henry VII not to admit the refugees from Spain: and still we read that there were many refugees from Spain in England in 1492. Henry VIII married his brother Arthur's widow, Catherine of Aragón, daughter of Ferdinand and Isabella, after his accession to the throne of his father in 1509. The sole surviving offspring was Mary Tudor, the second of four wives of Philip II, son of Charles. The young Charles visits Henry and his Aunt Catherine in the year of his coronation as Emperor of the Holy Roman Empire (1520) — a title to which Henry had aspired.

The Jews had appeared in England at the Conquest (1066). They became the personal property of the king, who shared their earnings. They prospered, subject to the common hazards they met in all Christian lands.

In 1254 and 1255 they appealed to the king to be allowed to leave England. In February, 1255, Henry III (1216–72) sold the Jews to his brother Richard, Earl of Cornwall, for one year for five thousand marks. (In the Great Interregnum of the German emperors between the reigns of Conrad IV of the House of Hohenstaufen and Rudolf I of Hapsburg [1254–73], Richard was crowned at Aachen [1257].)

The marriage of Nicole de Berechiah's daughter, Bellaset, was being celebrated at Lincoln in August, 1255, when the ancient libel was repeated. Ninety-one guests went to the Tower of London. Eighteen were executed for refusing to offer a plea and their property was forfeit to the king. (The estates of all usurers, Jews or Christians, fell to the crown at death.) Berechiah went free, but the rest spent the time in prison until Richard procured their release. Henry, in Lincoln a month after the affair, revoked the pardon granted the informer, had him dragged about the city tied to a wild horse, and then hanged.

The prioress in Chaucer's *Canterbury Tales* recites the legend of a young saint in an Asian city who passed through "the Jewerye" on his way to and from school singing—

O Alma Redemptoris Mater

Our firste fo, the serpent Sathanas
That hath in Jewes herte his waspes nest—

appealed to the Jews to avenge this slight to their Law. Even with his throat cut the lad sang "loude and clere."

At the close of the tale the prioress invokes the prayers of the rather recent English martyr:

> O younge Hugh of Lincoln, slayn also
> With cursed Jewes, as it is notable.

The elder saint, Bishop Hugh of Lincoln, the Carthusian monk, invited into England by Henry II, died in 1200, as sincerely mourned by the Jews as by his own flock.

Increasing restrictions, ecclesiastical and civil, left the Jews no place: they were banished by Edward I on July 18, 1290, and given until November 1, All Saints' Day, to leave. Not until Oliver Cromwell felt it expedient (1654) were they invited to return.

A deputation of prominent Maranos waits on Charles in Flanders to appeal against the inquisitor Adrian. (Maximilian had appointed Adrian of Utrecht to direct the education of his grandson Charles.) Adrian, Bishop of Tortosa, succeeded Ximenes as Grand Inquisitor of Spain (May 4, 1518). Adrian the Humanist, cardinal, vice-chancellor of the University of Louvain, professor of theology, Regent of Spain (1520), succeeded Leo X in 1522–23 as Adrian VI. When Adrian was Pope his personal physician was a Jew: he thanked the Jewish physicians at Rome for their work during the plague. Alexander VI (1492–1503) set the fashion of favoring his Jewish doctor—Samuel Zarfati. Succeeding popes renewed the special privileges of the family.

Leo X grants the Jews a protective bull, reaffirming their prerogatives, freeing them from inquisition and excessive taxation (November 1, 1519), following up the permissive bull of October 12, 1519. Charles through his envoy Hurtado lets Leo know that no bull restraining the Inquisition will be published in his domain. The complaints of a few Spanish bishops and others deserved no credence. The converts had offered him and his grandfather (Ferdinand) huge sums. The inquisitor Adrian would be only too lenient. It is generally believed that if the chancellor Selvaggio had lived, Charles would have moderated the Inquisition.

Leo X, Giovanni de Medici, Pope from 1513 to 1521, patron of learning and art, allows the establishment in Rome of a Hebrew printing press. The Babylonian Talmud is printed in Venice in 1520 and the less comprehensive Jerusalem or Palestinian Talmud is brought out there is 1523 by the same publisher, Daniel Bomberg. Leo's sympathies are evidently with the Humanist Reuchlin, promoter of Hebrew studies in the universities, in his long controversy carried on in pamphlets with the convert Pfefferkorn from Cologne, who represents the hostile German and Spanish clerics.

In the spring of 1531 John III urgently demands a bull of Clement VII authorizing an Inquisition. The opposition to such a tribunal is louder in Portugal and in Rome than it had been in the earlier grant to Spain. The Bishop Fernando Coutinho at home; the Cardinal Lorenço Pucci, who proclaimed his conviction that John wanted what Ferdinand and Isabella had wanted— the property of the Jews; the Cardinal Ghenucci, who wrote a book in defense of the Jews; the Grand Inquisitor, the Franciscan Diogo da Silva, confessor to John who balked at the post: the Papal Nuncio Della Ruvere: clearly represent the conscience of the Church as against the coercion of the state.

The Bishop Fernando Coutinho, councilor of the Supreme Court, replies to Emanuel on the idea of a forced baptism of the Jews (February, 1497): "No compulsion and persecution can make a sincere Christian out of a single Jew."

A Marano is accused of disrespect to Mary. The Royal Council sends the proof to Bishop Coutinho (1531). He refuses to pass judgment. The Maranos are to be considered as Jews, not as Christians:

> Even if I were not a man of seventy and were I more in accord with the present time, I would still pronounce the verdict to be false; since it is clear and evident that the law condemns it. The Provost who brought the action, and all the witnesses, ought to be tortured; for no witnesses are ever called that have not been bribed with money or otherwise. I will have nothing to do with the matter. I need not act the part of Pontius Pilate.

John has his bull from Clement in December, 1531. In 1532 John rules that no Jews are to leave Portugal: death is the penalty for the captain or owner of a vessel transporting them. Clement then issues the famous Bull of Pardon, April 7, 1533, in which he defines heresy. Forced conversions are not valid. One brought into the Church by his parents, even though he had been reared as a Jew, is to be considered as a Christian. The Inquisition was aimed primarily at converted Jews and at Judaizers who either reclaimed converts or proselytized among Christians.

Paul III continues the indulgence of his predecessor, Clement VII. Like Clement, he too favors his Jewish physician. Paul issues the Bull of Pardon of October 12, 1535, to all neo-Christians. Charles in Rome in April, 1536, after his victory at Tunis, asks Paul as a favor to grant his brother-in-law the Inquisition he desires. John has his bull from Paul in May, 1536: the trials must be conducted after the model of the civil courts, open and with the names of witnesses and accusers made known to the accused; for ten years the property of the condemned is to go to the natural heirs.

The Jews have the earnest support of the Papal Nuncio, Della Ruvere, in representing to the Pope the cruelty of John. The eloquent Marano advocate, Duarte de Paz, is now out of the way. The *conversos* address a memorial to the Pope asking for the repeal of the bull of May 23, 1536: They will be compelled to return to their Mosaic religion and to leave their old homes to live among less-cruel peoples. The Pope establishes a commission of cardinals, among them Jerome Ghenucci. A bull of February, 1537, in effect nullifies the Inquisition.

In February, 1539, a placard appears on the cathedral and church doors of Lisbon: "The Messiah has not come; Jesus was not the true Messiah." The "Lisbon Placard" was traced to a Marano—Manuel da Costa. (The false witness invited the fate of his intended victim.)

The ineffectual Diogo is dismissed. The Cardinal Infante Henrique, fifth son of Emanuel (who will succeed John's grandson Sebastian on the throne), is now Grand Inquisitor. The bull of October 12, 1539, which insists on fair procedures, is not published. On October 23, 1541, occurs the first public auto-da-fé in Lisbon.

In answer to the Jews of Hungary, Bohemia, Poland, Paul

issues the bull *Licet Judaei* (It is allowed the Jews), May 12, 1540—the blood libel is "invented to permit murder and robbery under the guise of religion." Paul issues the bull *Exhibita Nobis* in answer to the appeal of the Jews of north Italy, prohibiting the clergy to arouse the people against them.

The "Sacred Congregation of the Roman and Universal Inquisition or of the Holy Office," composed of six cardinals, is established by Paul in April, 1542. There is no mercy for the heretic in the Church. The Franciscan who would be a Jew, Cornelio de Montalcino, is burned alive in September, 1542, by Paul's order.

Paul continues his consideration to the Jews. He asks the Christians to be kind to the exiles from Sicily and Naples. The Papal Chamberlain admits Sicilian exiles to Ancona in 1543, requiring only that they pay the 5 per cent tax that the Jews are contributing to the Turkish War.

The Maranos address a memorial to the Pope, giving it into the hand of the sympathetic vice-chancellor, Cardinal Alexander Farnese, reviewing all they had suffered in Portugal to the present (1544). The Papal Nuncio, Luis Lippomano, has not arrived in Lisbon when letters appear discrediting the agents of the Maranos, the new Nuncio, and Pope Paul. The majority of the cardinals, including Paul Caraffa, are now with John. The bull of August 22, 1546, renews the bull of May 23, 1536, for one year. Cardinal Ricci, replacing Lippomano, delivers a rebuke to the inquisitors, the Cardinal Infante Henrique, and King John.

The Maranos appeal to John to effectuate the Bull of Pardon of October 12, 1535. John appoints a commission of four Maranos to formulate the conditions which they will accept. They answer: If peace were granted, the wanderers would return and revive commerce and industry. Even in Spain they are not ill-treated unless found guilty of some offense. Few will remain without tolerance. Those who flee are hospitably received in other Christian lands. The inquisitors reject the proposals. Now the Curia proposes a general pardon for all Maranos who publicly confess their allegiance to Judaism. The Bull of Pardon, dated May 15, 1547, is published in the Cathedral of Lisbon July 10,

1548. Soon after the neo-Christians pronounce their recantation before the Church of the Hospitalers and there is an interval of peace.

Paul IV (1555–59) "lived for the Holy Office." He enforced all previous restrictions and added to them. Jews were not allowed to practice medicine among Christians. Paul was especially zealous against Judaizers and against Hebrew books—the Talmud and commentaries, even the prayer book. While still a cardinal, Paul ordered the confiscation of all copies of the Talmud in the hands of Jews or Christians, forbade its importation from Turkish lands or reprinting in Christian countries. All Jews or Maranos arriving from Portugal were to be burned immediately according to the order of April 30, 1556. Twenty-three men and a woman arriving in May were publicly burned in Ancona: thirty-eight were sent to the galleys. When Paul died there was a riot in Rome. The inquisitors were roughly handled; the court documents were burned, and the prisoners released.

Sebastian (1557–78) allowed the Maranos to leave Portugal for the payment of 250,000 ducats.

Mary Tudor's fierce pursuit of heretics corresponded with the reign of Pope Paul IV. It will be recalled that Mary, sole surviving offspring of Henry VIII and Catherine of Aragón, was the second of four wives of Philip II. In the month of October, 1553, in which Mary was crowned in Westminster occurred the affair of Servetus at Geneva. The Spanish physician and theologian who had written on the errors of the Trinitarians, fleeing the Inquisition in France that Calvin had escaped earlier, was apprehended by the Church of the Reformers, and, after a trial which lasted from August 14 to October 26, and with the concurrence of other Swiss cities and leading reformers, among them "the gentle Melanchthon," Luther's co-adjutor, was burned at the stake October 27, 1553. Beza, the Humanist who succeeded Calvin as head of the Church at Genva, wrote in defense of the punishment of heretics by the civil magistrate.

Sébastien Châtillon (Castellio), theologian, Humanist, Bible translator—himself a deviationist in doctrine—published a pamphlet at Basle in 1554—"Ought Heretics to Be Persecuted?"—

renewing the plea for religious toleration which he had made in the dedication to the young Edward VI of his annotated Latin translation of the Bible (1551). It was still too early for the modern world to question the axiom "Whose the rule, his the religion" (*Cuius regio illius religio*).

Charles' son, Philip II of Spain, Philip I of Portugal, had claims to the throne of Portugal through his first wife, Mary, daughter of John III, son of Emanuel, and through his mother, Isabella, sister of John III and daughter of Emanuel. The Duke of Alva, who had fought Charles' battles for twenty years, defeated Antonio, Grand Prior of Crato, a grandson of Emanuel and last of the House of Aviz. Alva climaxed his victory at Alcántara (1580), then a suburb of Lisbon, with a general massacre as he had done in the conquered towns of the Netherlands.

Philip brought all the apparatus of the Inquisition to bear on the Protestant revolt in the Netherlands—lands that had savored liberty. In 1580, when the Duke of Parma was regent, Philip published a ban against William of Orange with a promise of gold and a title of nobility to his executioner, who accomplished his purpose in 1584.

The Duke of Alva, whose remorseless orthodoxy matched his king's, instituted a "Council of Blood" that in the six years of his regency (1567–73) rivaled in victims the modest assessment of the three hundred and fifty years of the Spanish-Portuguese Inquisition.

In the time of Pedro II, third son of John IV (the Duke of Braganza who restored the independence of Portugal, 1640), there was an extended effort to suppress the Inquisition. Pedro's tutor, the missionary Jesuit Antonio Vieira, himself victimized by the Inquisition at Coimbra, sought and won the ready sympathy of the Jesuit University of Coimbra and of the Popes Clement X and Innocent XI.

Clement's bull of October 3, 1674, was repeated by Innocent. The Inquisitor-General was to deliver to the Papal Nuncio within ten days all the documents of the courts. The inquisitors and a large part of the Cortes agreed with Pedro (then regent for his brother Alfonso VI) in desiring all to be as it had been. The

Inquisitor-General appointed by Innocent refuses to obey. The bull of August 22, 1681, opens a new series of autos-da-fé that, beginning with May 10, 1682, at Lisbon, equal any in the past.

The Inquisition in Portugal held its last auto-da-fé in 1765 in the reign of King Joseph Emanuel (1750–77). His reforming Prime Minister, Marquis de Pombal—who liberated the native slaves in Brazil (1755), suppressed the lists of neo-Christians in 1768, and removed all disabilities based on descent in 1773—in his battle with the Jesuits commends the Jesuit missionary to Brazil, the aged Gabriel Malagrida, to the traditional fate of the heretic in the auto-da-fé held at Lisbon in September, 1761.

Charles II, last of the Spanish Hapsburgs, lights the fagot that sets the fires of the grand exhibition at Madrid in June, 1680. His young wife is a spectator. Joseph Bonaparte abolished the Inquisition in Spain in 1808. Ferdinand VII re-established it in 1814, although the Cortes had condemned it the year before. The tribunal was closed by the Cortes in 1834 and the next year the assets were diverted to public uses.

Larned (III, 757) sums up the work of Ferdinand, Isabella, and Charles: "The Spain of their day had the fairest opportunity of any nation in Europe for a great and noble career."

ABRAVANEL

THE history of the Rabbi Isaac Abravanel (Abarbanel) illustrates the precarious involvement of the Jew in the political affairs of Europe. Abravanel was a member of one of the most eminent Spanish families and, in the carefully preserved Jewish genealogy, a descendant of King David. The family coat-of-arms is to be seen in the Portuguese synagogue at Amsterdam.

Abravanel was born in Lisbon in 1437, and died in Venice in 1508. His grave is in Padua. After the expulsion from Spain in 1492, Italy became the intellectual center of the Jews and Maimonides continued as their philosopher.

Abravanel was treasurer to Alfonso V of Portugal, as his father, Dom Judah, had been before him. Isaac's grandfather, Samuel, became a Marano in Portugal, but three years later publicly returned to Judaism, with the consequent loss of his fortune to the state. Alfonso was king at the age of six and reigned from 1438 to 1481. His conquests won him the title "the African." John II, "the Perfect," successor to his father (1481–95), in his campaign to crush the nobles accused Abravanel of having conspired with the Duke of Braganza, already executed. Abravanel escaped to Toledo (1483) in the year Torquemada was appointed Grand Inquisitor in Spain. In a six-month interval Abravanel wrote the extensive commentaries on Joshua, Judges, Samuel.

Abravanel entered the banking firm of Don Abraham Senior of Segovia, who was engaged in financing the Moorish Wars (1482–92). Segovia was a province of Old Castile. The capital, Segovia, a Roman city, was a residence of the kings of León and Castile. After the fall of Granada, Ferdinand issued the Edict of

Expulsion against Jews and Moors (March 31, 1492). Abravanel offered Ferdinand a great sum from his Jewish subjects; but although the royal treasury was depleted, Ferdinand did not relent, and Abravanel with his wife and three sons joined a company of exiles bound for Naples (July 30, 1492).

Ferdinand V of Castile (1452–1516), II of Aragón and Sicily, III of Naples, shared the throne of Aragón with his father, John II of Aragón and Navarre in 1466, and two years later was proclaimed King of Sicily.

In 1469 Ferdinand married Isabella. The nobles and junta of Segovia recognized Isabella and Ferdinand as co-heirs of Castile at the death of Isabella's brother Henry IV in 1474. Henry's will declared his daughter Juana his lawful heir. Supporting Juana and opposing the accession of Ferdinand and Isabella were the Grand Master of the Military Order of Calatrava, organized in the twelfth century for defense against the Moors; the Archbishop of Toledo; Alfonso V of Portugal; Louis XI of France, father of Charles VIII. Alfonso was defeated at Toro, Spain, in 1476. Later Ferdinand brought the headship of the three great chivalric orders under the crown.

Ferdinand's sister, Leonora de Foix, inherited Navarre at the death of their father (1479). The French king, Louis XII, cousin of Charles VIII, invaded Italy and took Milan. Maximilian I had married Bianca Maria, granddaughter of Francesco (I) Sforza (1493) and invested her uncle Ludovico Sforza with the dukedom of Milan, from which he was expelled by Louis in 1499. Navarre sided with Louis when the Holy League was formed against him by Pope Julius II with Emperor Maximilian, Ferdinand, Henry VIII of England, Venice, and the Swiss Confederation (1510–13). Louis was in the alliance against Venice in the League of Cambray (1508–10).

Ferdinand invades Navarre (1512) and in 1515 holds the four kingdoms of Spain—Aragón, Castile, Granada, Navarre and Sicily and Naples.

Louis had an anterior claim to the Sforza in the Visconti family. Gian Galeazzo Visconti, founder of the Milan Cathedral, acquired the dukedom of Milan from Emperor Wenceslaus of

Bohemia in 1395. Gian married Isabella, daughter of King John II (the Good) of the House of Valois. Gian's daughter, Valentina, married (1387) Louis, Duke of Orleans, brother of the French King Charles VI.

Louis XII, son of Charles, Duke of Orleans, is grandson of Valentina and great-grandson of Gian. Gian's granddaughter, Bianca Maria, heir of her father, Filippo Maria Visconti, married (1441) Francesco (I) Sforza, who became Duke of Milan in 1450.

Alfonso V of Aragón, I of Sicily and Naples (the Magnanimous), was designated heir to the throne of Naples by Joanna II (1414–35), who had his help against the invading Louis III of Anjou in 1420. Three years later she transferred her favor to the conquering Louis.

Joanna I of Naples (1343–81/82) had adopted Louis I, second son of John II of France, as her heir in 1380, passing over her previous choice of Charles of Durazzo, Charles III of Naples. Charles I of Naples (1266–85), Count of Anjou, youngest brother of Louis IX of France (Saint Louis, the Crusader) had been crowned King of Naples by Pope Clement IV.

Charles II of Naples, son and successor of Charles I, was progenitor of both Charles III and Louis I. From the three sons and two daughters of Charles II stemmed five royal and interrelated lines. Charles III takes Naples from Joanna in 1381 and defeats the counterclaimant, Louis I, in 1384. The antipope Clement VII at Avignon backs Louis' claim. Louis I and his son, Louis II, Louis III, and René, his brother, second son of Louis II, rule as titular heirs to Joanna I (d. 1382). The last, René (1435–42), is forced out of Naples by Alfonso.

Ferdinand I of Naples is son of Alfonso. Ferdinand II, grandson of Ferdinand I, is left to occupy the throne of Naples when his father, Alfonso II, who had alienated his subjects, abdicates his brief reign at the approach of the French king, Charles VIII, in 1495. Ferdinand V of Aragón with his general Gonsalvo expelled Charles and restored Ferdinand II to the Neapolitan throne, which he himself was to occupy in 1504 as Ferdinand III.

Abravanel, in the service of Ferdinand II, escaped with the king to Messina before Charles entered Naples. In Naples in 1495 Abravanel had completed his commentary *The Top of Amana* (Song of Solomon 4:8), in which he defended Maimonides and his "Thirteen Articles of Belief." He himself leaned toward the traditional 613 precepts, since each word of the Law is a divine revelation. Abravanel felt that Maimonides only followed the fashion in formulating a doctrine.

Abravanel made his way to Monopoli on the Adriatic coast. Here he wrote his three works on the Messiah, conceding Daniel a place among the Prophets instead of leaving the apocalypse in the third order of the Jewish classification—the Writings.

In 1503 Abravanel is in Venice. He is sent by the Doge of Venice to negotiate a treaty of commerce between the historic republic and the old despotism that first set his feet in the path of exile.

Judah Abravanel (Leo Hebraeus), eldest son of Isaac, was physician, poet, philosopher, in the grand tradition of the Golden Age. At the expulsion he was urged to stay in Spain and threatened with the loss of his year-old son Isaac to the Christians. Judah refused and sent the infant to Lisbon. There he was taken as a hostage. Judah laments his fate in an elegy written in Hebrew (1503) and addresses his boy, who would under his father's guidance be preparing to assume his obligation as a Son of the Commandment (a Bar Mizvah): "Remain continually mindful of Judaism, cherish the Hebrew language and literature, and keep ever before thee the grief of thy father, the pain of thy mother."

Judah wrote in Italian (1502) the graceful and much-translated *Dialogues of Love*. Philo, the Lover, converses with Sophia (Wisdom) in a humanistic blend of Greek myth and Hebrew allegory. Judah was physican to Gonsalvo, Ferdinand's general and viceroy of Naples, until Gonsalvo's dismissal (1505–7), when Judah sojourned in Genoa.

Joseph, the second son of Isaac Abravanel, had a career as physician and scholar in Venice and Ferrara.

Samuel, the youngest son, was born in Lisbon in 1473 and

died in Ferrara. Samuel was treasurer to the viceroy, Pedro de Toledo, at Naples. Benvenida, wife of Samuel and teacher and companion to Pedro's daughter, Leonora, succeeded in deferring the execution of Charles' decree of expulsion in 1533. Years later Charles[1] set the Jews the alternative of wearing the badge or leaving Naples. Samuel and Benvenida went to Ferrara.

It is said of Isaac Abravanel that in all these vicissitudes he neither complained nor exulted—truly a religious philosopher.

---

[1] Charles I of Spain (1516), Charles V of the Empire (1519-56), a grandson of Ferdinand and Isabella.

CHRIST AND BUDDHA

THERE is a significant parallel in the lives of Christ and Buddha. The conditions of birth are similar: the divine dispensation, the annunciation, the immaculate mother. The prognostics of the Buddha include miracles of healing like the signs of the Messiah. Those in bonds are freed. Nature is redeemed. "The light that never was on sea or land" irradiates the worlds.

The birth stories from the Introduction to the Jataka are more extravagant than the apocryphal tales of the infancy, which at points they resemble. Lumbini Grove, where the future Buddha was born, becomes a heavenly scene like the cave in the Gospel of the Infancy. In both there is an angelic guard about the Mother and the Child.

The first sight of human misery, one example of wretched age, of disease, of death, awoke the divine nature in the young prince. He left the luxury of an oriental palace, his lovely wife, Yasodhara, and infant son, Rahula, to try the adventure with God. His last appearance as a prince and his first entry into the city of Rajagaha in the new character of mendicant monk were triumphs.

The next six years were a great struggle, fruitless in result. Gautama[1] was abandoned by his five monastic companions when he decided that asceticism was not the Way. Then the body, emaciated and blackened with rigors, was transfigured to its former radiance. At the sacred place in the River Neranjara the future Buddha performed his lustrations before assuming the robes of sainthood.

[1] *Gautama* in Sanskrit, *Gotama* in Pali, the sacred tongue of the Buddhist scriptures. *Siddhartha* in Sanskrit, *Siddhattha* in Pali; *Nirvana* Sanskrit, *Nibbana* Pali.

Gautama was about thirty-five years old when he formed the mighty resolution: "Let my skin, and sinews, and bones become dry, and welcome! and let all the flesh and blood in my body dry up! but never from this seat will I stir until I have attained the supreme and absolute wisdom!" Seated in the immovable position of contemplation, with his back to the trunk of the great Bo Tree of Uruvela, facing east, he was assailed by all the hosts of Mara, god of the sensual world, while ten thousand worlds looked on and offered homage.

With the conquest of Mara (Death), Gautama became "the Enlightened One"—the Buddha. Born of Maya (Illusion), his given name Siddhartha means "successful in his objects." His patronymic Sakya means "the powerful." Sakyamuni was "the Solitary of the tribe of Sakyas." Buddha continued in the sacred spot, "the Throne of Wisdom," fasting for forty-nine days, completely engrossed in the new doctrine.

He had rejected the succor of gods in the Great Struggle. Now the milk rice of which he partook on the eve of Enlightenment, into which the gods had infused a divine essence as the devoted Sujata prepared it, sustained him with heavenly food.

Then the obligation presented itself of imparting the new doctrine to the world. He thought of his teachers, but they were gone. He recalled the five monks who waited on him in the years of struggle. There was in him no resentment, no anger, for anger was unknown to him, only gratitude for the service they had done him. He went to them to announce that he had found what they all sought: "The door stands open to the Deathless."

After a ministry of forty-five years he died at peace, attended by the constant Ananda, his last word delivered to the assembled order: "And now, O priests, I take my leave of you; all the constituents of being are transitory; work out your salvation with diligence."

He does not leave them comfortless; the Doctrine and Discipline are to be their Teacher when he is gone.

To both Christ and Buddha death was the shadow always resting on the loveliness of life. This abomination of darkness they penetrated with a living light. They made death beautiful. The loss of the present world was the gain of the heavenly one.

They taught religion, not ethics or philosophy, and brought the hope of a common human brotherhood to the outcasts of a priestly society and a larger vision to the privileged. They opposed a simplicity of life to the current ideal of asceticism. They manifested a boundless compassion. Jesus left his heavenly home, Buddha delayed his entrance into Nirvana, to serve mankind.

Their desire was to give the world one beautiful gift. They had one purpose, the cure of souls, and one subject—salvation. A confession of faith was the only passport to Heaven. It was an exacting allegiance, nevertheless, requiring the complete surrender of the will, the intellect, the imagination, the affections. The enlightenment of faith carried the compulsion to spread the truth; for to both Christ and Buddha the Truth is one.

"I am the Way, and the Truth, and the Life: no man cometh unto the Father but by me."

The Fourfold Truth and the Eightfold Path alone conduct to "rebirth beyond death in the blissful Heaven world," or to "the fruit of not returning." The Kingdom of Heaven, or Nirvana, is present with the saved, but future in the fulness of realization.

Women were among the earliest and most faithful followers of Jesus. They were in the missionary band that came with him out of Galilee. Only at the intercession of Ananda did Buddha yield an unwilling consent to the founding of an order of priestesses.

The woman in the Gospels whose act of homage Jesus commends to the remembrance of all calls up the story of Buddha's meeting with his wife after many years as a holy man—the wife whom he had not bade farewell. In utter worship she prostrates herself and lays her hands on his feet, then rises and stands aside to let him pass. (He is not hers but God's.)[2]

The doubt of God's Providence Jesus answers characteristically with a call to repentance. The Galileans massacred by Pilate and the people crushed by the tower of Siloam were not greater sinners than others.

---

[2] W. E. Soothill, *The Three Religions of China*, p. 82.

Buddha explains by his central doctrine, Karma, how Moggallana the great disciple could have met an unworthy death. It was the crime of a previous existence. Sariputta and Moggallana found Buddha as Andrew and Peter found Jesus. Peter was given the keys of Heaven and Hell. Moggallana aroused the enmity of the other sects by ascertaining from those in Heaven and Hell their Karma and teaching the Law of Causation.

The pervasive charm of both teachings lies in the illustrative story that enforces the deep moral. Both Christ and Buddha expressed a distaste for the supernatural. (No man knows these things. The wicked seek the sign from Heaven.) The source of their power was prayer. Jesus was instant in communion with the Unseen Reality. The meditation of Buddha was a withdrawal from the sensory world into the subliminal self, the superconscious self. Through prayer they overcame the world.

They who refused a universal earthly sovereignty hold undisputed sway over the hearts and the imaginations of men. From the heights of spiritual achievement, towering above a world of sin and misery and death, the refuge of weary multitudes, two mounts of blessing, they speak the one victory, the other peace.

PAUL AND FELIX

PAUL before Felix reasoned of righteousness, temperance, judgment—of ethics. The fugitive religious impulse he aroused was soon overcome by the habit of worldliness. Paul appears before a modern Felix, philosophically as thorough a skeptic as the Roman, in religion as affirmative as Paul himself.

There is a close kinship of spirit in these two representatives of the Hebrew genius, in their constant moral purpose, in their religious passion.

Paul declares to the Sanhedrin: "I have lived in all good conscience before God until this day" (Acts 23:1). The Apostle of the Moral Life validates his claim for each one: "The moral end is an infinite end . . . superordinated above all other finite ends whatsoever." In the crisis of their lives, when they could no longer in conscience defend the faith into which they were born, then for conscience' sake they gave themselves to the new; for as Felix Adler put it, "The fount of revelation is not sealed."

Felix Adler reaffirms natural as against supernatural sanctions. ("And what saith the Scripture? 'The word is very nigh unto thee, in thy mouth and in thy heart' "—Deut. 30:14; Rom. 10:8.) Matthew Arnold in *Literature and Dogma* bases the world's regard for the Jewish revelation securely on the "facts of human nature and on the unalterable constitution of things." The modern apostle's business is ethics. Like Paul, he does not wish to "trespass or seem to trespass" on his neighbor's domain.

He dreads the imputation of Pharisaism, of being called a "whited sepulchre," as he expounds from his own experience the rules for ethical living—as he "lifts up a standard for the people" (Isa. 62:10; Jer. 50:2; cf. I Cor. 9:27). But ethics must submit to the test of empiricism, with power as sharp as the two-edged sword of Scripture to cut the user.

Here too is a prophetic mission. "I felt myself to be the channel of a spiritual principle that operates in and through men. What strength I have had has been derived from that. All the influence that I ever exercised is due to that." Felix Adler expressed himself as grateful for the Idea that had used him.

So much for God's part . . .

Its human counterpart is the initial deep-felt need—"the sense of personal need, the inextinguishable longing, the desire to end the intolerable, internal discord, to gain deliverance from the sense of the futility of human life, from inevitable self-contempt. The problem of how to gain deliverance from this evil plight stands in the foreground." ("O wretched man that I am! who shall deliver me from the body of this death?"—Rom. 7:24.)

The Holy Thing is the God in man, with a shift in emphasis from the divine Being to the divine life. To most minds God is the Charioteer holding the reins (as in the Upanishads the mind [the self] is the charioteer holding the reins of the senses).

Felix Adler disclaims the pantheism that might appear to a superficial eye in his Ethical Manifold, which supplants the One of the Hebrews, as he claims that Paul's ethical conception of man also prevents more than a hint of it in his theology (I Cor. 15:28; Col. 3:11).

Pantheism easily relates the finite to the infinite. God is all and in all. But to Felix Adler there is a practical dualism between the physical and the moral order. How the two can exist side by side is unknowable. A veil impenetrable to man is between. But we assume that the imperfect, the finite, exists to be put in fee to the perfect, the infinite. We cannot construct a bridge between the mortal and the immortal. An impassable gulf divides them.

To Paul also there is a division between the temporal and the eternal, the seen and the unseen. But if the earthly existence is dissolved there remains its eternal counterpart with God. The earnest desire of the finite creature is that it may not be divested of its mortality, but invested with immortality, or, in other words, that the finite may be dissolved in the infinite according to the divine purpose. The Holy Spirit is the bridge between the two worlds. The veil of mystery that Felix Adler does not hope to lift Paul finds to be done away in Christ. As always, Paul stresses the divine Being, as against the "divine life."

The eternal communion of essential selves is God to Felix Adler. ("Henceforth know we no man after the flesh"—II Cor. 5:16.) Paul believes that though in the present knowledge is partial, yet when the perfect shall have succeeded the imperfect, all things will be known.

The quest for the Eternal is formulated in the Upanishads: "Lead me from the unreal to the real! Lead me from darkness to light! Lead me from death to immortality!" (*Brihadaranyaka-Upanishad* I.3.27.)

The new ethical religion is related to Judaism and Christianity. In Judaism the holiness principle in man, his moral nature, gives him worth. Judaism separates between the evil and the good. The ruling concept is justice, with its corollary, mercy. The Christian would separate the evil from the good in his own heart. The main concept is purity, its concomitant Christian love, best demonstrated by imbuing another with the faith (James 5:20). Christian purity is the effort to maintain self-identity against disintegrating forces.

The spiritual nature is defined as worth, from the Hebrew holiness; as uniqueness, from Christian individualism—the assertion of "the irreducible intactness of the spiritual part of man"— as organic. Felix Adler uses Paul's metaphor to describe his own sociological, his group, ethic. Corresponding to the members of the Church constituting the body of Christ, the vocational groups are defined as the organs of the true organism, true because the parts are necessarily related, of the eternal, spiritual society. All functions must be on a level with respect to the worth of those who exercise them—equivalence rather than equality. Not heads and hands and feet in the body politic, but all personalities with heads and hearts. (Paul sets the example after the Master of being hand as well as head and heart.)

The dependence on others for the satisfaction of wants may be social rather than ethical, as Aristotle relates the Greek master to his slave. Paul returns the runaway slave to his master as a brother and as his own son to be freely released. We have a right to the services of others, but none over their personality—a right that Paul finds it expedient to forego in order to prove that his aim is not dominance but helpfulness. No one serves his own or another's material wants, but the master, the god in himself and in the other. ("And whatsoever ye do, do it heartily, as to the Lord, and not unto men"—Col. 3:23.)

How shall I love my neighbor?

Spiritually a man can have no enemies, since each is potentially a member of the spiritual society—a neighbor near or far. "Thou shalt love thy neighbor, not as thyself but as other than thyself, a part of thy life which is in him and not in thee." The principle is extended to national and international relationships. ("Even as I please all men in all things, not seeking mine own profit, but the profit of many, that they may be saved"—I Cor. 10:33.) Felix Adler drew to the ethical leadership men from such diverse traditions as John Lovejoy Elliott and Henry Neumann.

There is a mutuality of salvation. "The ethical consideration is that the vitality that is in you shall not be the death of that which is in your fellow." Read Paul on idols (I Cor. 8:10; Rom. 14). ("Through thy knowledge shall the weak brother perish, for whom Christ died?")

The true temperance is the positive elevation and transformation of desire. ("And the life which I now live in the flesh I live by the faith of the Son of God"—Gal. 2:20.) The prize of life is growth, change ("Changed . . . from glory to glory"—II Cor. 3:18.)

Recognizing the danger of such a figure as living or dying in another being taken for natural human sympathy, Felix Adler points out that the spiritual living in another is to become a spiritual entity oneself. ("I am debtor both to the Greeks and to the Barbarians"—Rom. 1:14.) It is a rebirth such as Jesus

describes to Nicodemus (John 3:1 ff.). "Was there ever a more
consoling, a more inspiring message uttered since the human race
began?"

In working out the ethical ideology, New Testament terms
come most easily to hand, especially the Pauline. Salvation
ethically depends on being in a new sense "a people of the Way."
Felix Adler calls the bread of the moral life his Eucharist, nor does
he exclude any from that table. He loves to think of the raising
of Lazarus and reflect on the raising of the spiritually dead. Can
religion be revived and revive us, the spiritually dead? Craving
for resurrection from the death-in-life of futility, he seeks to evoke
the god, the numen, in others. He serves not the body of that other,
itself a servant, but the master—the spiritual end.

Like Paul he strives for the supreme "prize," to reach the
"goal." (Phil. 3:14; I Cor. 9:24.) His statement of aim has
an ancient Brahmanic tone: "Whoever standing on the earth as
a foundation builds up for himself the spiritual universe attains
the purpose of human existence." The world as we know it is
the veil, translucent at the point of ethical experience, of the
spiritual universe (II Cor. 3:13–18; 4:6).

A thorn in the flesh each of us is inevitably in his neighbor's
side, like the messenger of Satan that kept Paul humble. And still
eternal worth is held in the frail vessel of mortal existence—"the
treasure in earthen vessels." The light of ethical perfection is to be
reflected from the face of human society. The future stretches
out its arms and makes us willing servants.

The life work of man is to burnish a mirror to reflect ever
more clearly the divine reality, an eternal world of communion
of essential selves. Now we see merely the shimmer of the spiritual
reality of things.

It would be interesting to see which of the two men used the
words *spirit, spiritually,* more often. "Spirit is one of the potencies
of being." "Quench not the Spirit" (I Thess. 5:19). Jesus taught
that all things are forgiven unto the sons of men, but a sin against
the Spirit of Holiness—a sin against the Spirit of God which is the
Spirit in man—is not forgiven—not ever. Felix Adler also finds

"edification" in the rugged sense of upbuilding too valuable a word to lose. Knowledge may puff up, but the true *caritas*—dearness (the ascription of worth)—builds up (I Cor. 8:1).

Sadly Felix Adler rehearses his frustrated aspirations, the points of his life at which he knew the crucifixion. He gathers the spears of frustration into his breast to make a way for liberty. It is when pain is left unrelieved that there comes the peace that "passes understanding" (Phil. 4:7). ("My grace is sufficient for thee.") "For these cruel spears turn into shafts of light radiating outward, along which my spirit travels, building its final nest—the spiritual universe."

Like Paul, Felix Adler brought all things into the circle of the sovereign Ideal. An ethical leader must not exhibit his own intellectual accomplishment; he is as a ministrant before the altar. ("For we preach not ourselves"—II Cor. 4:5.) Paul's goal was "the high calling of God," Felix Adler's a human society transformed and transfigured by the application of universal spiritual law in human relations—the prophetic ideal of social justice.

What is it to which, like Paul, Felix Adler says, "Yea and Amen," and that redounds "unto the glory of God by us"?

The ideal of perfection has its counterpart in the ultimate reality of things.

There is an eternal divine life beyond imagining ("above all that we ask or think"; cf. Eph. 3:20).

The divine life continues all that is best in each. ("The gifts and calling of God are without repentance"—Rom. 11:29.) Since all that is dear to him is contained in that divine life, he is able at last to bless the universe—and that is life's supreme prize. "I bless the universe" is his Amen.

Like Paul, Felix Adler had an original theory of sin and the law.

Evil is evil before the deed; but it is sin after the deed, when the doer is made aware, by his own revulsion of feeling, of the holy laws against which he has offended, of his own failure, of his hindering the task of mankind. "Godly sorrow working repentance" (II Cor. 7:10). The subsequent enlightenment brings the sense of the intrinsic holiness of his own nature ("that sin by the commandment might become exceeding sinful"—Rom. 7:13). The process of self-condemnation and rebirth is the expiation, the repentance. "Must I then do evil in order to gain the enlightenment?" ("Shall we continue in sin that grace may abound?" —Rom. 6:1; 3:8.) The question is idle. Everyone stands convicted of sin. But it is possible to improve the inevitable occasion to spiritual advantage. "Of our vices we can frame a ladder." ("The publicans and the harlots go into the Kingdom of God before you"—Matt. 21:31.)

Jesus on the Cross prayed: "Forgive them." He had faith in his enemies. "Open their eyes, that they may see the light," is Felix Adler's interpretation. Forgiveness can only follow on repentance. Faith is help to effect the change of heart. Forgiveness records the change. It is not to forget, but to recognize the essential divine in oneself and in the other. It is a miracle like that at Cana when the water of earth becomes the wine of Heaven.

Paul never told the whole vision. He retained his reticences.

Did Felix Adler's austerity veil the ineffable loveliness of the Ideal with which he was wont to commune?

Felix Adler felt that the Jewish and Christian systems were closed, incapable of further expansion or reinterpretation. Did he not himself show a way?

("Can religion be revived and revive us, the spiritually dead?" . . . " 'The moral end is an infinite end . . . superordinated above all other finite ends whatsoever.' " . . . "Felix Adler calls the bread of the moral life his Eucharist, nor does he exclude any from that table.")

Bishop Manning said, "The Bible has been studied too much." Jesus asks only that he be heard. The prophet is advised to write so that he that runs may read. Paul acknowledges his indebtedness to Greeks and to Barbarians, learned and unlearned (Rom. 1:14). A fresh "look at the Book" may revivify what has grown tedious to many.

"Other sheep I have, which are not of this fold [aulé]: them also I must bring, and they shall hear my voice; and there shall be one [flock (*poímne*)][1] and one shepherd [*poimén*]." Mary Baker Eddy, with a grim religious background, and with no profound scholastic training, after years of struggle succeeded in restating the affirmations of the gospel.

Felix Adler took high ground in his criticism of the old ways; but still, like Paul, in his missionary zeal he was a little unjust toward the great past. Neither Judaism nor Christianity was as ungenerous in its inception as the narrowing influence of the centuries makes it appear. Each was a large vision of life, the proclamation of a new liberty.

Felix Adler is impatient with "that perfectly empty word— 'the One.' " Still, it had its connotation to others than the Jews. He objects to the cultivation of moral qualities, such as righteousness, because a holy Being has commanded them, and to the emphasis on the divine Being instead of the divine life. All this constitutes an indirect approach to the Eternal, as in all old religions. Justice, Truth, Right, are holy in themselves and by their own nature work salvation. *God* is a provisional term. "The idea of God has served as a picture or image, enabling us to think the thought of this vast, endless universe."

If Felix Adler left Judaism behind, he found the Christian faith untenable. Neither can be abstracted from its setting—the prophetic state, the "One," and the apocalyptic vision. Both are circumscribed. His objections to the Christian religion are the confession of impotence, the appeal to mystery for salvation, the flight to mysticism from reasonable experience. Hebrew monotheism precluded his Ethical Manifold—that universe conceived in the mind of man, made up of the manifold of all human existences. Christianity centered around Christ, who had not spoken the last word on ethics, although he was an original and incomparable teacher. His message is to recognize the evil in your enemy as in your own heart and to triumph over it in yourself.

---

[1] Not "fold," as in A. V. (Westcott and Hort, *The New Testament in the Original Greek*.) See translations of John 10:16 in James Moffatt, *A New Translation of the Bible*, and in Richard Francis Weymouth, *New Testament in Modern Speech*, 3d ed.

"Mystic, metaphysician, moralist," wrote the enthusiastic young disciple, Henry J. Golding, in his copy of *An Ethical Philosophy of Life,* placing his master in that great company of brothers among whom the most eminent in spirit is accounted first.

BIBLIOGRAPHY

Arnold, Matthew. *Literature and Dogma.* James R. Osgood & Co., 1873.

Barth, A. *The Religions of India.* Trans. J. Wood; 5th ed. London: Kegan Paul, Trench, Trübner & Co., 1921.

Barton, George A. *Archaeology and the Bible.* 7th, rev. ed. Philadelphia: American Sunday School Union, 1937.

Breasted, James H. *The Conquest of Civilization.* N. Y.: Literary Guild, 1938.

Brown, Brian. *The Wisdom of the Egyptians.* N. Y.: Brentano's, 1923.

Drummond, James. *Philo Judaeus; or, Jewish-Alexandrian Philosophy in Its Development and Completion.* 2 vols. London, Edinburgh: Williams & Norgate, 1888.

Finegan, Jack. *Light From the Ancient Past.* Princeton: Princeton University Press, 1946 (repr. 1949).

Frazer, James George. *The Golden Bough.* 1-vol. ed. N. Y.: Macmillan, 1922, 1935.

Gilson, Etienne. *A History of Christian Philosophy in the Middle Ages.* N. Y.: Random House, 1955.

Inge, W. R. *The Philosophy of Plotinus.* 2 vols. N. Y.: Longmans, Green & Co., 1918. The Gifford Lectures delivered at St. Andrew's, 1917–18.

Larned, J. N. *Larned's History of the World; or, Seventy Centuries of the Life of Man.* 5 vols. World Syndicate Co., 1915.

Lea, Henry Charles. *A History of the Inquisition in the Middle Ages.* 3 vols. 1888. The best-known work on the Inquisition in English: the *Catholic Encyclopedia* refers to "the much-vaunted impartiality of Lea."

Mills, Lawrence. *Our Own Religion in Ancient Persia.* La Salle, Ill.: Open Court Publishing Co., 1913.

Moore, George Foot. *History of Religions.* N. Y.: Charles Scribner's Sons, 1926. A volume of the International Theological Library.

Nilsson, Martin P. *A History of Greek Religion.* Trans. from the Swedish by F. J. Fielden. London: Oxford University Press, 1925.

Ottley, R. L. *A Short History of the Hebrews to the Roman Period.* N. Y.: Macmillan, 1915.

Pater, Walter. *Plato and Platonism.* London: Macmillan, 1912. First published 1893.

Peel, Robert. *Mary Baker Eddy: The Years of Discovery.* N. Y.: Holt, Rinehart and Winston, 1966.

Schechter, Solomon. *Studies in Judaism,* Series I. Philadelphia: Jewish Publication Society of America, 1896. The first of three series.

Soothill, W. E. *The Three Religions of China.* 2d ed. London. N. Y.: Oxford University Press, 1923.

Spaeth, J. D. *Old English Poetry.* Princeton: Princeton University Press, 1922. Source of the lines quoted from the "Elene" of the *Saints' Legends.*

Weber, Albrecht. *The History of Indian Literature.* Trans. from the 2d German ed. by John Mann and Theodor Zachariae. London: Kegan Paul, Trench, Trübner & Co., 1904; popular ed., 1914.

Zeller, Eduard. *Aristotle and the Earlier Peripatetics.* Trans. from his *Philospohy of the Greeks* by B. F. C. Costelloe and J. H. Muirhead; 2 vols. London, N. Y.: Longmans, Green & Co., 1897. The comment on Alexander's purity of character appears in vol. I, p. 23.

TEXTS (PRIMARY SOURCES)

Adler. Felix, *An Ethical Philosophy of Life.* N. Y.: D. Appleton & Co., 1918.

————. *The Reconstruction of the Spiritual Ideal.* N. Y.: D. Appleton & Co., 1924. The Hibbert Lectures delivered at Manchester College, Oxford, in May, 1923.

————. Quotations in the last essay were taken from reprints of his speeches that appeared in various issues of *The Standard* for 1933 and later.

Ambrose, Bishop. Epistle to Theodosius. In *Nicene and Post-Nicene Fathers,* 2d Series, X, 450 (epistle 51). N. Y.: Christian Literature Co.; reprinted, Grand Rapids: Wm. B. Eerdmans Publishing Co.

Ante-Nicene Fathers. Ed. Alexander Roberts and James Donaldson; 10 vols. N. Y.: Charles Scribner's Sons, 1899 ff.; reprinted, Grand Rapids: Wm. B. Eerdmans Publishing Co., 1951 ff. Esp. Vol. I: "Apostolic Fathers, With Justin Martyr and Irenaeus."

Apocrypha and Pseudepigraph of the Old Testament: The Apocrypha According to the Authorized Version. Ed. R. H. Charles. Oxford, 1913, 1963. The Apocryphal Old Testament: fourteen books in the Septuagint and the Vulgate, not in the Masoretic canon. The Pseudepigrapha (technically in another's name): books classed below the deutero-canonical, from the two centuries before and after Chirst.

Aristotle, *The Basic Works of.* Trans. W. D. Ross; ed. Richard McKeon. 1 vol. N. Y.: Random House, 1941.

Confucius. *See* Legge, James.

Darmesteter, James, trans. *Zend-Avesta.* In *Sacred Books of the East,* Vol. IV: Part I, *Vendidad;* Vol. XXIII: Part II, liturgy. Oxford, 1985, 1895.

Euripides. *The Bacchanals.* London: J. M. Dent & Sons; N. Y.: E. P. Dutton & Co. The play is also known as *The Bacchae* and *The Bacchantes.* (Quotations in the text are from the earlier translation in the Everyman Library, not from the more recent version first issued by Everyman in 1956.)

Eusebius, Church History of. In *Nicene and Post-Nicene Fathers,* 2d Series, Vol. I; trans. Arthur Cushman McGiffert. N. Y.: Christian Literature Co., 1890; reprinted, Grand Rapids: Wm. B. Eerdmans Publishing Co., 1952. Covers A.D. 1–324. For Eusebius on Josephus and the authenticity of his accounts, see book III, chapters 9 and 10.

Eusebius. *Preparation of the Gospel. See* Philo Judaeus.

Gathas, The. See Mills, Lawrence.

Halevi. *See* Judah Halevi.

Hesiod. *The Poems and Fragments.* Done into English Prose by A. W. Mair. London, N. Y.: Oxford University Press, 1908. Contains *Works and Days* and *Theogony.*

Holy Bible, The. Authorized Version. *See also* Moffatt, James; Weymouth, Richard.

Holy Scriptures According to the Masoretic Text, The. A new translation with the aid of previous versions and with constant consultation of Jewish authorities. Philadelphia: Jewish Publication Society of America, 1917, 1955.

Homer, The Iliad of. Trans. into English blank verse by William Cullen Bryant; ed. and abridged by Sarah E. Simons. Boston: Houghton Mifflin Co., 1916.

————. Done into English prose by Andrew Lang, Walter Leaf and Ernest Myers. London: Macmillan, 1883.

Homer, The Odyssey of. Trans. into English blank verse by William Cullen Bryant. Boston, N. Y.: Houghton Mifflin Co., 1871.

————. Done into English prose by S. H. Butcher and Andrew Lang. N. Y.: P. F. Collier & Son, 1909. First published 1879.

Homeric Hymns. A new prose trans. by Andrew Lang. N. Y.: Longmans, Green & Co.; London: George Allen, 1899.

Ibsen, Henrik. *Emperor [Caesar] and Galilean.* In two parts; Part One: *Caesar's Apostasy.* London: Walter Scott Publishing Co.; N. Y.: Charles Scribner's Sons.

Josephus, Flavius. *Antiquities of the Jews, Wars of the Jews* (first published in Hebrew), *Against Apion.* Trans. William Whiston; 2 vols. London: Chatto and Windus, 1912.

Judah Halevi. *The Book of the Kazars.* Trans. from the Arabic by Hartwig Hirschfeld. London: George Routledge & Sons; N. Y.: E. P. Dutton & Co., 1905.

Koran, The. Trans. from the original Arabic by George Sale; 2 vols. London: Longman, Rees & Co., 1836.

Legge, James, trans. *The Chinese Classics,* in seven volumes. Vol. I: *Confucian Analects, The Great Learning, The Doctrine of the Mean;* Vol. II: *The Works of Mencius.* Oxford, 1893, 1895.

————, trans. *The Texts of Confucianism.* In *Sacred Books of the East,* Vol. III, Part I: The Shu King and The Shih King. Oxford, 1899. "The Book of History and The Book of Poetry."

————, trans. *The Texts of Taoism.* In *Sacred Books of the East,* Vol. XXXIX, Part I: Tao Teh King ["The Way and Virtue Book"], and Vol. XL. Oxford, 1891.

Leo I (the Great). Epistle to the Bishop of Asturias in northern Spain, A.D. 447. In *Nicene and Post-Nicene Fathers,* 2d Series, Vol. XII, pp. 20-26 (epistle 15). N. Y.: Christian Literature Co.; reprint, Grand Rapids: Wm. B. Eerdmans Publishing Co. On the Priscillianists.

Maimonides, Moses. *The Guide for the Perplexed.* Trans. from the original Arabic text by M. Friedländer; 2d, rev. ed. London: George Routledge & Sons; N. Y.: E. P. Dutton & Co., 1936.

Max Müller, F., trans. *The Upanishads.* In *Sacred Books of the East,* Vol. I, Part I; Vol. XV, Part II. Oxford, 1900.

————, trans. *Vedic Hymns.* In *Sacred Books of the East,* Vol. XXXII, Part I. Oxford, 1891.

Mencius. *See* Legge, James.

Mills, Lawrence, trans. *The Gathas.* In *Sacred Books of the East,* Vol. XXXI. Oxford, 1887.

Moffatt, James, trans. and ed. *A New Translation of the Bible.* N. Y.: Harper & Brothers, 1935.

Nicene and Post-Nicene Fathers: A Select Library of the Nicene and Post-Nicene Fathers of the Christian Church. 1st and 2d Series, 14 vols. each. N. Y.: Christian Literature Co., 1890 ff.; reprinted, Grand Rapids: Wm. B. Eerdmans Publishing Co., 1952–56. *See* Ambrose; Eusebius; Leo I; Saint Augustine; Theodoret.

Philo Judaeus, The Works of. Trans. from the Greek by Charles Duke

Yonge; 4 vols. London: H. G. Bohn, 1854–55. Vol. IV contains the collected *Fragments,* including those preserved in Eusebius' *Preparation of the Gospel* (pp. 210–42).

Plato, The Works of. Trans. Benjamin Jowett; 4 vols. in one. N. Y.: Tudor Publishing Co.

Sacred Books and Early Literature of the East. Ed. Charles F. Horne, with a staff of specialists; 14 vols. N. Y., London: Parke, Austin & Lipscomb, 1917. The superscription to the Code of Hammurapi on page 13 is quoted from I, IV, 114, *Letters and Inscriptions of Hammurapi,* translated by L. W. King. The Psalm and Lament cited on page 20 are in I, VIII, 251 ff. and are taken from J. M. Jastrow, *The Civilization of Babylonia and Assyria.*

Sacred Books of the East. Ed. F. Max Müller. Oxford, at the Clarendon Press; republished, Delhi: Motilal Banarsidass, 1966. *See* Darmesteter, James; Legge, James; Max Müller, F.; Mills, Lawrence.

Saint Augustine's City of God. Abridged and trans. by J. W. C. Wand. London, N.Y.: Oxford University Press, 1963. Also in *Nicene and Post-Nicene* Fathers, 1st Series, Vol. II; trans. Marcus Dods.

Saint Augustine, Confessions of. In *Nicene and Post-Nicene Fathers,* 1st Series, Vol. I. N. Y.: Christian Literature Co.; reprinted, Grand Rapids: Wm. B. Eerdmans Publishing Co.

————. Trans. Edward B. Pusey. Oxford, 1838, 1843. A volume of A Library of Fathers of the Holy Catholic Church Anterior to the Division Into the East and West.

Theodoret. His account of Ambrose meeting Theodosius before the basilica in Milan in A.D. 390. In *Nicene and Post-Nicene Fathers,* 2d Series, Vol. III, book V, chapter 17.

Upanishads, The. See Max Müller, F.

Vedic Hymns. See Max Müller, F.

Warren, Henry Clarke, trans. *Buddhism in Translations.* Cambridge: Harvard University, 1896. Vol. III of the Harvard Oriental Series.

Westcott, Brooke F., and F. J. A. Hort. *The New Testament in the Original Greek.* New York: Macmillan, 1937.

Weymouth, Richard Francis. *The New Testament in Modern Speech.* Boston: Pilgrim Press; London: James Clarke & Co., 1909. Now available in a more recent edition from Harper & Row (N. Y., 1951).

Zend-Avesta. See Darmesteter, James.

REFERENCE WORKS

(These standard reference works have not been cited as sources for specific data in the text of these essays. They were used throughout, but especially in collecting material for the second and third essays, "The Middle Years" and "The Inquisition.")

Catholic Encyclopedia. N. Y.: Robert Appleton & Co.

Dictionary of Events. N. Y.: G. P. & G. H. Putnam; G. P. Putnam's Sons, 1890, 1907–27; Grossett & Dunlap, 1936. In various revisions, with new material added.

Ferm, Vergilius, ed. *An Encyclopedia of Religion.* N. Y.: Philosophical Library, 1945.

Hastings' Encyclopedia of Religion and Ethics. N. Y.: Charles Scribner's Sons, 1914.

Hughes, Thomas Patrick. *Dictionary of Islam.* Clifton, N. J.: Reference Book Publishers, 1965. (A reprint.)

Jewish Encyclopedia. N. Y.: Funk & Wagnalls Co.

New Catholic Encyclopedia. 1907–14.

New Standard Bible Dictionary, A. N. Y., London: Funk & Wagnalls Co., 1926.

Universal Jewish Encyclopedia. Universal Jewish Encyclopedia Co., 1939.